DAN

(I'll be, You'll be, Y'all be)

WITH EXCERPTS FROM

LETTERS TO THE

PRESIDENT (10/13/08 -6/15/10)

(And many insightful views into the ReCorpiCon's relentless march to form a Fascist Government)

By

Turnin A. Hausround

Lulu Book Publishing

To the honor and the services of the extended

Joseph Biden family

In the past, present and the future

and, to the tranquil memory of the past.

Copyright @ 2010 by Lulu Book Publishing

All rights to copies reserved and Liability Limited

Knowledge of or reading any part of this work limits Legal Liability of all kinds including tort / court to the max. and total extent of a refund of the current price of the book or document only. This means the intender understands and agrees from the knowledge of this work or book from the outset that there can be no initiation of any legal action, tort / suit against any entity associated with the writing, publication, printing or distribution of this work, book or document. Copies may be produced only by permission.

Printed in the United States of America

Designed by and Thoughts by the Author

Published by Lulu Book Publishing

USA

Library of Congress Cataloging - in - Publication Data

Hausround, Turnin A., Letters to the President, Corporate Strangle Hold, Scourge, Diary, Fascism, Health Care, Jobs, Retirements, ReCorpiCon, Capitalism at Worst

(10/13/08 to 6/15/10) / Turnin A. Hausround - 4th ed.

A Book by: Lulu Book Publishing

ISBN: 978-0-557-52831-8

PREFACE i

<u>DAMNED</u> (I'll be, Y'all be) Being President. (10/08 - 6/10)

It was the Best of Times, It was (NOW) the Worst of Times

Twas the Winter of our Discontent made Glorious Summer

After the contentious campaigns – both primary and the presidential - it's become painfully clear that even the <u>best of intentions</u> of those "<u>for</u> WE THE PEOPLE" <u>have been gleefully diminished</u> by the ReCorpiCon's Scourge. <u>What seemed clear by WE THE PEOPLE as a revolution to take back our government</u> has painfully <u>become a testament to how far the ReCorpiCons have taken total control and moved our fragile existence right into TOTAL FASCISM</u>!!!

<u>Since the country's been under constant, various attacks on it's ability to SURVIVE</u>, the <u>ReCorpiCons have done NOTHING TO PROTECT- WE THE PEOPLE - instead worked constantly TO DESTROY the present government</u> and it's <u>ability to protect WE THE PEOPLE</u>!! Every <u>catastrophe</u> has become <u>a battle cry for Political VICTORY</u> <u>rather than a humanitarian concern to solve real problems facing America</u>. A comment made by an <u>oil filled congressman shows just how far</u> these ReCorpiCons are <u>committed to protecting the huge, reckless Corps that feed them</u> rather than deal with real life situations. <u>This proves the totally callus disdain and regard for those who have been severely damaged by the worst environmental disaster of all time</u>! Even more, <u>the comment shows a complete disregard for the Small Business interests the ReCorpiCons so often tout as the basis of AMERICA'S FUTURE GROWTH</u>!!

These notes were <u>written</u> on the indicated dates and are apropos to what was going on at the time. They're considered a diary about the ReCorpiCons and the complete damage they have caused. They serve to

ii. <u>show the fallacies and hypocrisies of their claims through the actions they take daily and the other words and statements they make</u>. Insights of the writer show the insensitivities to those stuck out here on the receiving end in the "other" America. So many <u>terrible things</u> – have happened since Nov. 4th 2008. No better way to show them than to use the <u>time capsule</u> of the notes that had been written to bring some perspective and sense of reality back to what had been said, felt and promised during the campaigns. They're a unique view into the future and what we should do to <u>prevent future FASCISM</u>!!

Some of the "considerably, before the fact" suggestions are appearing to be extremely relevant at the time the book is being published. In hindsight, it seems that some of them are perhaps portentous and future predicting!! Things might have been very much better had what had been suggested been implemented. <u>Hopefully, congress will finally decide to get serious about the real problems created over the past decade</u> and get down to <u>doing the PEOPLE'S business getting this Nation back on track</u>!!!

The way it's been going one doesn't seem to need Bin Laden or anyone else to make problems for America. <u>ReCorpiCon POLITICS has TAKEN CARE of that distasteful prospect, very well</u>! This has been a huge awakening for the 200 million of us <u>out here</u> struggling <u>to keep</u> a living and a house over our heads and trying to avoid getting sick to avoid losing whatever <u>little else we may have left</u>!!! <u>Forget about retirement, it LEFT long ago</u>!!! Perhaps this book will give some insights into the nature and basis of the ReCorpiCon caused problems <u>and, hopefully, thus provide insight into ways to ROLL BACK TOTAL FASCISM</u>!!!!

CONTENTS iii

Democratic Convention, Denver, CO. 8/25/08 – 8/28/08

Sarah Palin announced as VP Candidate Fri. –   8/29/08

Republican Convention, St. Paul, Minn. 9/2/08 – 9/4/08

First Presidential debate – 9/26/08   –   Oxford, Miss.

Vice Presidential debate – 10/2/08   – St. Louis, Mo.

2nd Presidential debate – 10/07/08 – Nashville, Tenn.

Last Presidential debate – 10/15/08 – Hempstead, NY.

CHAPTER 1	10/13/08	1
CHAPTER 2	10/15/08	3
CHAPTER 3	10/21/08	7
CHAPTER 4	10/26/08	9
CHAPTER 5	11/04/08	13
CHAPTER 6	11/10/08	14
CHAPTER 7	11/17/08	18
CHAPTER 8	11/18/08	20
CHAPTER 9	11/23/08	22
CHAPTER 10	11/25/08	26
CHAPTER 11	12/11/08	28
CHAPTER 12	12/25/08 - Xmas!	30

Iv CHAPTER 13	01/01/09	- New Years!	34
CHAPTER 14	01/09/09		36
CHAPTER 15	02/28/09		38
CHAPTER 16	03/09/09		40
CHAPTER 17	06/19/09		42
CPAPTER 18	07/19/09		45
CHAPTER 19	08/29/09		49
CHAPTER 20	09/19/09		50
CHAPTER 21	11/04/09		51
CHAPTER 22	11/22/09	Thanksgiving	52
CHAPTER 23	12/25/09	Xmas!	53
CHAPTER 24	01/11/10	After New Year	55
CHAPTER 25	01/25/10	State of the Nation	59
CHAPTER 26	02/04/10		66
CHAPTER 27	02/16/10		71
CHAPTER 28	02/23/10		74
CHAPTER 29	02/28/10		75
CHAPTER 30	03/08/10		78
CHAPTER 31	03/23/10		88
ADDENDUM BASED UPON EVENTS TILL 6/15/10			100

AS TO THESE ELECTIONS PLEASE FOCUS ON AND v. REMEMBER THESE THINGS AND ONLY THESE!!!

1. <u>THIS IS NOT ABOUT THE</u> NAME OR FACE OF <u>PERSONS</u> THAT ARE <u>RUNNING</u> BUT RATHER<u> ABOUT: HOW ARE YOU GOING TO PREVENT FURTHER FASCISM</u>! ASK:
2. WHAT DAMAGE DID YOU SUFFER IN 8 BUSH YEARS?
3. WAS THIS COUNTRY BETTER OFF IN 8 BUSH YEARS?
4. IS THIS COUNTRY RESPECTED WORLD WIDE MORE OR LESS THAN IT WAS 10 OR 2 YEARS AGO?
5. ARE WE SAFER THAN BEFORE 8 BUSH YEARS?
6. CAN YOU AFFORD TO HAVE THREE ULTRA CONSERVATIVE JUDGES ADDED TO THE SUPREME COURT THAT WILL ABSOLUTELY CHANGE YOUR LIFE IN A WAY THAT YOU WILL NOT BE ABLE TO CHANGE – OR HAVE ANY CHOICES IN LIFE FOR YOURSELF OR HAVE ANY VOICE TO CHANGE IT OR RESIST THE EFFECTS FOR PERHAPS THE NEXT 40 TO 50 YEARS?
7. CAN YOU AFFORD TO HAVE THIS ENDLESS WAR KEEP TAKING RESOURCES FROM FAR MORE CRUTIAL ENDEAVORS LIKE REDUCING THE DEFICIT?
8. CAN YOU AFFORD TO HAVE YOUR SALARY AND RETIREMENT DWINDLE DOWN TO NOTHING AS IT DID DURING THE PAST ReCorpiCon DECADE?
9. ARE YOU READY TO BE BANKRUPTED BY HUGE CONTINUED MIGRATIONS TO TOTAL FASCISM BROUGHT ON AND SUPPORTED BY ReCorpiCons?
10. CAN YOU AFFORD TO WORK TILL YOU DIE?
11. THIS ELECTION HAS ABSOLUTELY NOTHING TO DO WITH THESE PEOPLE WHO ARE RUNNING, BUT MORE ON THE ReCorpiCons vs <u>YOUR VERY URGENT LIFE, JOBS, COMFORT AND RETIREMENT NEEDS!!!</u>

DEDICATION

Dedicated to a Democracy in Mourning

- For Itself - AND

To a Nation that suffers at the hands of the ReCorpiCons

FAR, FAR TOO Patiently

and

Surprisingly and FOOLISHLY TOO Calmly

AND

To the People who are Suffering Needlessly

and Seemingly – Endlessly

AND

To all Others who Need and Deserve a Dedication

and

Who Are Not or Will Not be likely to Receive One.

And to the other books by Turnin A. Hausround

<u>Letters to a (Would be) President</u>

<u>Letters to a (Trying to be) President</u>

<u>The Corporate Scourge</u>

<u>The Corporate Strangle Hold</u>

CHAPTER 1

<u>DAMNED</u>   Letter to the President 10/13/08

A very simple message today. I saw you speak in Ohio and McCain speak in W. Virginia this morning. McCain is finally talking about the economy. CNN presented you first.

Do you know that commercial where one person is talking over the other person with a slight delay, but mimics the first by saying the same thing? That is what we are seeing in the campaign now!! But in this case with a huge difference – you presented a plan with specifics and details and time lines and talked about difficulties and budgetary concerns and how it will be paid for. McCain talks in glowing, wondrous platitudes, using words calculated to evoke the strongest emotional responses, words that say little of how or where it will be paid for and almost nothing about details or specifics of how it will be implemented. He relies on words of "honor" "strength", "judgment" "no need for training", "years of service" etc. to "sell" his case for being the best "choice".

When it has become clear that both campaigns are now using and talking about the same thing – mirror images of each other – seemingly both inventing the message of change, both using the message of how to fix this economy, both promising to be the agent of change – it may appear to the "non critically thinking" public that they are in fact running for the same thing on the same ticket – with one being "stronger" than the other to do exactly the same thing.

2   It is at times like this to get back to basics and let it be known and that it needs to be reinforced - which Group got us into this mess, which Group, (ReCorpicons), stole our jobs, our houses, our savings, our future incomes and which Group, seems intent on continuing to do the same. I have emails - from Orin Hatch and others (Chamber of Commerce) - that say, they need to WIN to keep what has been started and implemented by Bush to remain and to keep going - the Bush Tax Cut, Control of the Government, selection of Conservative Judges for the Supreme Court and to break the firewall in Congress. I don't know how else to say it, but at last look despite the Sheep's Wool, both McCain and Sarah are both of that Group! McCain voted 90+% times with Bush when in fact had he chosen to use his conscience, he could have and should have voted against Bush's agenda and the Group line thus clearly supporting his claim and giving credence that he is truly a "Maverick"!!

Keep it simple, keep the message of not only change, but exactly what that change will look like, how it will be implemented, and where the money will come from. McCain is still trying to claim that your tax is a "tax hike for all" and <u>for small businesses</u>. However, he is still part of a ReCorpicon Group and it was the ReCorpicons who got us into this mess and took our money and future and seemingly fully intended to do more of the same to get the very last DIME of not only us, but our children, grand children and great grandchildren!! They seem to be on the way with the TARP bill and the outrages that we are now seeing. THIS CANNOT BE ALLOWED TO HAPPEN!!!!

CHAPTER 2

<u>DAMNED</u>   Letter to the President 10/15/08 Last Debate

Great Debate. It is certainly clear that you won resoundingly. You could have nailed the McCain health plan by stating a <u>tax credit</u> requires an <u>income</u> to be worth anything and then only a small percentage of the actual value of the $5,000. To be of any value, then, one has to have a job and pay taxes. Besides, money is needed every month to pay for insurance - not as a possible tax reduction a year later if you pay taxes.

I notice Cindy sitting behind McCain at his rallies appears to be wistfully looking hundreds of miles away as if saying - "John, why don't you give this crap up and lets go home to Arizona. Hell, you must know you have lost this one and we might as well not spend the next 21 days wasting our time and money but instead let's go enjoy our pool and friends." When she claps, it seems to be a gesture of a clap completely devoid of any feeling.

Sarah seems to have had her hands "slapped" as she seems to be standing behind McCain looking on is if dejectedly. When she walks in front of McCain as she did at the convention, he seems to act as if to say, "get thee behind me Satin - I really don't want to see you anymore." It seems to be an interesting body language, wouldn't you say? It always seemed to me as if she may be entirely expendable and now she seems to be beginning to realize that she has not only been used, but had as well. She might have figured out long ago that her 15 min in the sun might be little more than that and may not lead to anything more than a ride back to Alaska.

4   You will perhaps recall, that I said that it should be back to basics – it's the ReCORPicons, stupid, it *is* the ReCORPicons. Tonight's debate should underscore that point over and over. It seems obvious that this theme and attack may be far more important in the next three weeks!! It appears McCain voted 90% with Bush in the past 8 years. His "tax" plan seems to continue Bush's tax cut for the rich and make it permanent. The list goes on and on, and you know far better than I the extent of the list of options to side with Bush. To counter he might say "Obama, I know George Bush and I, sir, am no George Bush". (paraphrased) Well, some Maverick. His claim to being a Maverick seems to fall into the realm of taking your campaign and trying to seem that it was his first. Oh, I almost forgot, he did pick the gift that keeps on giving.

Back to basics. The line should be that what has been done *to* America in the past 8 years may have been planned by a ReCORPicon Group. The operative word is – the ReCORPicon group. The literature they're sending out and using to try to put fear in their base is that the Democrats are planning to "Take over the government". This seems odd because it seems to be just like what they may have planned to do themselves. No wonder there is paranoia, they should not only know the "name" of the game but the means and the ends of it as well.

The question, then, that you should ask over and over again from now on is: "Well, have you had enough of what they have *done* *to* *you* in the past 8 years? Would you care for one more day of their agenda, let alone 4 more years? How well has it worked for you so far?" You should hear a resounding -- not at all Well!! A disaster!!

We are living in constant fear and with little or no income, no houses, and now having to have our kids, grandkids, great grandkids etc. bail out the Richest Financial Institutions, Banks and their executives after they essentially bankrupted America. You have got to be kidding – the vote should be 95 Obama, 5 McCain – but, Oh Yes, McCain claims to be a Maverick riding in on a white horse from the North to save America from what else? Oh, Golly Gee, The ReCorpicons?! <u>The real Meat</u>:>!

The last time I looked, McCain and Sarah <u>seem</u> to be ReCorpicons – oh yes, the very same ReCorpicons that took America from a 4 trillion surplus to a 4 trillion dollar deficit. OK, say we give him the benefit of the doubt and say he is a Maverick? How much? Perhaps he is only 50% as bad as the ReCorpicons that he Represents. WOULD YOU PREFER TO HAVE EVEN 50% OF THE TROUBLE YOU'VE HAD IN THE PAST 8 YEARS added for even one more day? I DON'T THINK SO!! Let's give him even a great deal more benefit of the doubt - say he is only 10% as bad as the Group he represents. Would you like even only 10% of the trouble and bad news that you have lived through piled on for even one more day? I DON'T THINK SO!!! Even 1% OF THAT NONSENSE IS TOO MUCH MORE TO ENDURE! ENOUGH IS SIMPLY FAR MORE THAN ENOUGH!!!

<u>New Jobs, technologies and new Renewable Energies:</u>

Next big issue to bring up. You talk about new renewable energy and it's effect on jobs and the economy. California, Oregon, Seattle, the Science triangle in the SE, Boston, Texas, etc. are (or were) centers for technology

6   development in the 80's and 90's. We now have a lot of those bright (brilliant) men and women working at places like McDonalds and Starbucks. <u>Potentially</u> there again can be huge salaries and tax bases for the states and federal government. During Clinton's early years, he used DARPA (later ARPA) with then reasonably small grants to a couple dozen companies like Tektronix, HP, Sarnoff and others to develop display and computer technologies leading to the super computers, laptops, TFT flat panel displays that made Laptops possible, HDTV and digital TV that will be the standard on Feb 17th 2009.

Some people I know worked on a number of those projects that led directly to the development of these breakthrough technologies and they worked closely with DARPA during those years to co-ordinate and plan future technologies and end concepts. They worked as well, on the technologies that led to the Cell Phone phenomena that we now all enjoy. I know that it can be done, work again and that there are the people there and available who can put it together to make it work early in your first term. What an income and tax base builder. (Like the Enigma code project in England)

One needs to start talking about how the <u>real</u> job recovery will begin and by what means that process will or may start, who implements it and how it will and how soon it can bring back the new breakthroughs throughout America. Those are and will become the high end high paying jobs of the new future that will prime the pump to take the deficit back to a surplus as it did in the Clinton years. It <u>is the change that we can do</u> and now very soon and early in your first term!!

CHAPTER 3

<u>DAMNED</u>   Letter to the President 10/21/08

Back to basics. The line might be "what has been done <u>to</u> America in the past 8 years may be the result of the carrying out of the Group plan of the past two decades". The operative word is – THE GROUP. Now what they seem to be using to try to put fear in their base is that the Democrats are planning to "Take over the government" - which ironically seemed to be what they seemed to have been planning for so long and very nearly succeeded. Is it no wonder they seem paranoid, as they seem to know the "name" and the ends of that game.

The question that you must ask over and over again is: Have you had enough of what <u>has been done to you</u> in the past 8 years? Would you like one more day of <u>that</u> agenda, let alone 4 more years? How about this last ploy of taking the last of the middle class dollars for 3 generations to come and giving it – <u>no questions asked and little to no conditions applied</u> - to the richest of the people, banks and institutions in this country? Oh Yes, He claims to be a Maverick and he is not Bush. However, he's still a ReCorpicon and his campaign <u>is</u> and agenda <u>will be</u> controlled by ReCorpicons. Yes, he's a Maverick – but a <u>Maverick from what and by how much</u>?

Let us give the benefit of the doubt and say he is a Maverick. Ok, how much of a Maverick is he? Perhaps he is only 50% similar to Bush or the Group that he represents. Would YOU PREFER TO HAVE SOMEONE WHO IS 50% LIKE BUSH FOR THE NEXT 4 YEARS - OR EVEN ONE DAY? I WOULD HOPE THAT YOU WOULD NOT THINK SO!!

Ok, Give him a lot of the benefit of the doubt - say he is only 10% similar to Bush or the ReCorpicons he represents. Would YOU LIKE TO HAVE SOMEONE WHO IS 10% LIKE THOSE WHO GAVE US THESE EIGHT YEARS TO LIVE THROUGH piled on for even one more day? I DON'T THINK YOU WILL FEEL SO!!! Even ONE PERCENT OF THAT NONSENSE SEEMS WAY TOO MUCH MORE TO ENDURE! ENOUGH JUST SEEMS TO BE WAY TO MUCH -- ENOUGH!!!

This argument is so powerful, because it honors the "claim" of Maverick while pointing out consequences of <u>what that really means to America with him still being a ReCorpicon</u>. A Maverick only means that some part of him will still follow the Group line. Even if he does only 1% of what his Group wants him to do, he is still going to do some of what they have done to <u>all of us</u> in 8 years – INCLUDING, ironically, TO MOST RECORPICONS AND INDEPENDANTS – as well as TO ALL AMERICANS EXCEPT the 5% making the top incomes and salaries.

And talk about the claims of Socialism – ie. taking money from the rich and spreading it around bringing good for all. Or perhaps spreading the wealth around for the benefit of all. On balance isn't it far better than - <u>taking money from the poor and middle classes and spreading it around to the richest 5% to 10% of the population</u>!! What might you call that? You might call it the <u>inverse Robin Hood</u> Syndrome. But it might be a better thing to call it A TRAVESTY AGAINST ALL AMERICANS!! PERHAPS ONE MIGHT CALL IT A TRAVESTY AGAINST THE PEOPLE OF THIS NATION - THIS THING WE CALL A DEMOCRACY!!

CHAPTER 4

<u>DAMNED</u>　　　　　　　Letter to the President 10/26/08

This argument is so powerful, because it grants the "claim" of being a Maverick while pointing out what <u>that might mean for America</u>. A Maverick only means some part still follows the Group line. If this is "so good" for Joe, the Plumber, why is so much going for big oil, medicine, big insurance and the rest of the LARGEST, richest, corps. in America? Those don't seem to be where Joe the Plumber works or may even want to work!!!

It's a funny thing about these down turns that I have noticed over the past recent three. The last was after the first gulf war after a period when things were rosy with a vibrant growing economy and led to a collapse almost immediately afterward. During the war things were going so well that companies had to triple order stock in order to get what they needed to make product. When the economy turned, these triple orders got canceled and that resulted in the inevitable spiral collapse. What contributed to change the equation so dramatically and rapidly was <u>a very small change in perception</u>. One has to ask: if all it takes to ruin a vibrant growing economy is a small negative change in perception, then why won't a creative small positive change in perception change it back to a vibrant growing economy just as rapidly?

The answer to that is simply – Yes it can and does if done skillfully and quickly. Bill Clinton must have known this when he inherited HW Bush's economic dilemma. He used DARPA very effectively (about a 100 million dollars is all it took -just peanuts in this administrations numbers)

10   to pump prime to get US businesses to re-invest in what was needed – new developments in computing to bring initiatives back to the US from Japan and Asia.

The first part of a <u>change in perception</u> would be an <u>Obama</u> win - that would be a big plus for America -as basically the reason you two are running so successfully is that you are for that "change in perception"! The new technologies in energy are the NOW needed new developments/products that need immediate pump priming. Only a billion dollars should get that pump primed nicely. (By the way, don't short change NASA as the developments that they produce also contribute to new technologies and products.) Blethley Park, England in WWII spurred numerous technologies and products.

We have all the talent needed available now just sitting around being wasted working at Starbucks etc. (perhaps a metaphor, but not far from the truth). We need to get these people back to doing very productive work building our economy and future. <u>However the process needs to be started almost immediately</u>. Just after winning the election, you must insist on a liaison office in the White House to start planning toward that goal. They should let you do that, and just why? They should be anxious to do that because they desperately need part of the credit to save a small bit of their "Legacy". (And a phrase comes to mind: "Beggars can't be choosers".)

You must get your team together NOW getting measures through congress and in Government agencies that will stimulate the economy by any means - even if it requires more "losses" for a short time. You have to <u>WASTE some heat and fuel first in order to build a ROARING FIRE</u>!!

You have to push through a monetary stimulus for 80% of America – <u>even it they don't have jobs or have paid taxes</u>. You have to <u>deal now</u> with the Mortgage crisis and housing – it must be reversed ASAP – no joke. You may even have to set up "refugee" camps like after the Tsunami or Katrina etc. We are that close to that kind of a catastrophe in the lower and middle classes in America. <u>The big Tsunami and Katrina may have affected a million people, but this disaster</u> that was caused <u>will effect 10's to 100's of millions of the USA in a horrendous way</u>. We are right now living in a kind of surreal, grotesquely suspended, <u>living hell</u> with <u>the other shoe not yet dropped</u>, but about to drop on any number of particular days very soon!!! They drop one at a time.

You have to start a kind of a WPA program to help those totally jobless without a clue of where to get a job anymore, working on public projects – from as simple as clearing ivy out of parks to full blown public works projects. This gives those totally hopeless <u>feeling</u> people a "job" and a place on a resume to move up to more responsible and more lucrative jobs when they become available. <u>Mark my words</u>, if you don't think this is necessary today, you will realize that this <u>was</u> necessary within a month or two – based on our present situation and economy – <u>it may then be too late to get started to be very effective when needed</u>! You may have to start a program to <u>pay</u> for the training (or college) plus a per diem for living to train those that are deemed trainable to compete and contribute in the newest technological

12   industries. You may call it whatever, <u>but it will pay dividends 100 times over</u>. Public service in return may be required as a requirement. <u>This has to start right NOW!!!</u>

After the Second world war, Europe and Japan had the luxury of being rebuilt with new factories, new technologies, new equipment and designs while America was stuck with old stuff that they could not justify replacing since they were still producing wealth – albeit not as effectively or efficiently as their competitors in Europe, Japan and Asia. We severely paid the price for that with Japan's JIT and Zero defect manufacturing.

This catastrophe is a blessing in disguise as you don't have to tear down institutions to rebuild them, but rather to rebuild the ones that they conveniently have torn down for you. For example the USBC has to have real teeth, not the milk toast pablum that the banks are paying it to mete out. Otherwise, you might eliminate all National banks - again making them State controlled banks so they can be effectively regulated and monitored at the local level. When they were State Banks, state regulators and District Attorneys had <u>real</u> jurisdiction over their business practices and <u>then</u> effectively kept them as true servants of their client base. The main part of this previous equation was that these monitors kept bank business practices sane and running with minimal risks. Overdrafts were discouraged but now under the National Bank system <u>overdrafts</u> seem to be <u>encouraged</u> and have <u>become a very lucrative source of income for these banks – almost one third of their total profits -- or about $33 Billion a year</u>.

CHAPTER 5

<u>DAMNED</u>   Letter to the President 11/4/08 - Victory!

Congratulations to you both!! Boy am I exhausted – but vindicated! I am so overjoyed that I have finally lived to see highly intelligent family men, statesmen, honest politicians, hard working insightful public servants, spokes persons, the ultimate role models for your professions, embodied in you and Joe Biden, stand on the stage that's long been deserved! Unfortunately, my boss died suddenly last Wednesday and was denied his opportunity to see this. I am so glad that I am here to witness this change for the better for him and will be, hopefully, able to finally begin to enjoy it with the World.

What a squeaker. All that rhetoric from the McCain camp in the last few days began to look like they were getting through to someone in Ohio and Pennsylvania. You were right to stay the course to the end and play out the game plan – just like Joe Pa. (even though I just learned that he was for McCain – and that almost ended my admiration.)

What you should have said and could still say to McCain is the following: "Well, John, with your new found passion for change, for main street vs wall street and all your promises to be an instrument of change, to regulate the financial institutions, banks, etc and to shake up Washington DC and it's old ways of doing business, defeating lobbyist etc. - <u>then I know that I can count on you</u> to be my bastion for change in the Senate to spear head America's plans and agendas in Congress and help usher them through all the opposition!!" "Thank you!!"

CHAPTER 6

<u>DAMNED</u>   Letter to the President 11/10/08

Yes, there is only one government and one president at a time – that goes without saying, but it would have been better to not say it almost apologetically Friday and again by Rahm Emanuel on Sunday! His appearances seemed embarrassing for you to say the least! That exposure seemed to be totally useless as there was absolutely nothing positive that he could say. He just looked foolish and totally ineffective. Not a very good beginning to making the best impression on a new start!

Again, beggars cannot be choosers. Bush needs something, <u>anything,</u> to fix his seemingly in the toilet legacy! At this 11th hour he should seem grateful for anything to seem like he did <u>something</u> for the real people of the United States – the middle and lower classes - those who produce the wealth that those upper 5 to 10% enjoy so much. It must be clear to Bush that there is a mandate to fix the results of the past 8 years and it must start changing now, <u>not starting January 21</u>. First up, Bush needs to be firmly pushed to approve an immediate stimulus package of 1-2 thousand dollars to everyone making under $80,000. <u>That needs to be passed by the congress this week and checks going out before Xmas!</u>. <u>Take it out of the $350 billion already approved</u> for the richest in the US. The <u>unemployment payments</u> have to be <u>extended immediately</u> for another 18 weeks minimum and there has to be <u>an immediate fix to those losing their homes</u> – like a <u>90 day moratorium on foreclosures</u> – hell, <u>we are bailing out the banks with our</u>

<u>hard earned money, they can sure wait to foreclose on the people's houses who are bailing them out!!</u> You don't need to be president to get these things started and done. Some pressure on Bush and on the congress should be all that is needed to get these things done. Those in congress need to have something to save their legacies. They are part and parcel to the disaster and need to be vindicated!! Get the Maverick, the change artist, the compassionate man for main street, the reformer to spearhead his buddies in the congress to follow through on what he promised so freely during the campaign!! After all, he was to be the "agent of change" not so? <u>Cheap words need immediate action for validity!</u>

Yes, I see that the WPA like effort has again been mentioned. Good, but not all workers are trained to do construction of infrastructure. We need to get the high paying jobs started ASAP and that means high tech work on alternate energies. Before being president, you and your working staff and those sympathizers in congress can start a Manhattan Project like effort to start finding and identifying Physical Chemists to start working on catalysts to concentrate and convert energy producing substances. Biologists and Biochemists are needed to work on enzymes and bacterial agents that concentrate and convert common substances like sugars from vegetation (all common vegetation) into high energy content fuels as well as help eliminate toxic waste and convert non useful substances to useful energy products. Carbon concentrating- conversion substances are needed to reduce CO pollution. <u>Mandate</u> has to be strongly pushed to stop the final days of the Bush disaster

16   from happening. He has to be told in no uncertain terms that no deals can be made, no pardons can be given, no treaties or agreements with IRAQ can be signed in the next 71 days without your approval. He effectively is no longer the president for the future even though he resides in the White House.

It has not yet been a week since the momentous election. If I am not mistaken, though it is clear that I could not have seen all the news or images of that night, but I did not see Hillary or Bill involved with any of the celebrations anywhere. Pity!

Oh, the transition. We all hope that you, like Bill Clinton, select very intelligent and well qualified advisers, staff, and cabinet members. We counted on that when we voted for you. We do not want any more "you're doing a hell of a job, Brownie" like selections. Apparently, when you are born with a silver spoon in your mouth" like it appears many prominent ReCorpicons seem to be, they seem to feel that Authority comes simply from a "title" or position. "You are head of Homeland Security, - therefore by fiat, you are by definition, not only the authority, but you are totally qualified to run that post". BS. Like Sarah who was "appointed" to be the VP running mate – it seems abundantly clear that more than "that title" was needed to make her fully qualified to fill that post. Examples might be found throughout the Bush administration – Gonzalas and perhaps others comes to mind. It sure is refreshing to see an intelligent president-elect working into the White House with a meaningful, intelligent, thoughtful, studied and deliberate transition.

We seem to have been deliberately dummied down far too long and on purpose. Science, education and manufacturing, & logic have been deliberately minimized and marginalized. We have set a new path to the lowest standard in education in the world and are being far outstripped by Pakistan, Russia, India and China etc in these areas of science and engineering. The huge danger in that – beyond the obvious one of losing market share in product development – is that we would not be able to mount an effective war against any of these places by losing our technological advantages in warfare armament developments as we have. Isn't it lucky atomic bombs aren't as easy to make as conventional bombs. Just contemplate about that now!!

We have lost or are about to lose our technological advantage in these areas and certainly have lost our ability to build these weapons in our shredded industrial complex. There's no way that we could fight a war with China if they are building our weapons. A metaphor of course. The stem cell mess is a prime example. With that one executive order, most of our stem cell experts left for other countries who are taking the initiative and will hold the lion's share of patents and reap the monetary benefits of those technologies to be developed.

Back to the transition. It appears that even with you there might be politics as usual, in that close friends may be the ones you are selecting. I sure hope that Biden doesn't become the next Colin Powell in this administration. Not liking what I am seeing so far but I sure hope that I am wrong. It seems like we are seeing a lot of ex Clinton-ites and DC Cronies.

CHAPTER 7

<u>DAMNED</u>   Letter to the President 11/17/08

Perhaps, <u>these two months are going to be the most important months of your entire presidency</u> – not yet the president, you might feel powerless to do the things you absolutely need to do to save this country from <u>total financial ruin</u> and save your presidency! <u>January 21 is far too late to do what is absolutely necessary NOW</u>!!!

What I am talking about is more important than putting together a cabinet or a white house staff – which you seem to be "busying" yourself doing to keep out of the way of the real issues. We elected you to be pro-active - <u>we expect you to be pro-active</u> and cannot tolerate and don't understand an Obama that is doing nothing more than politics as usual! <u>We are hurting out here, and we are going to hurt a HELL of a lot WORSE if the auto industry goes down</u>!! Especially if this happens before Xmas. You just got cushy jobs, ones we would kill to get our hands on, but we instead have to Try to Find <u>Any</u> Job to help <u>pay for yours</u>. <u>There just isn't much left out here anymore to do that and what is left is disappearing very fast</u>!

The opposition seems to have <u>learned absolutely nothing from this election</u>. They act like they did right after Katrina – freely spending 12 billion a month in Iraq for six years - they balked at voting $40 billion on restoring New Orleans. This <u>specious argument</u> about Detroit being irresponsible and not future looking and not deserving to be <u>loaned</u> money to avoid going bankrupt is ludicrous in light of the $700 billion they gave to the richest in the Banking, Finance and Insurance institutions in the nation!!

The original bill proposed by Paulsen was only 3 pages – a <u>blank check</u>!!! It was voted down by ReCorpicons on Wed. in the house when it was <u>only 180 pages.</u> Were they waiting for the <u>535 page</u> bill <u>adding $150 billion in pork barrel spending</u> on Friday when they voted for it to pass? <u>What hypocrites</u>!! I guess that it is good to bail out the most irresponsible, richest people in the nation with huge salaries, bonuses, perks <u>and parties</u> but not 10 million <u>hard working Americans</u> who may happen to belong to a union and only have ordinary salaries with little or no perks. An industry like that <u>effects 10 jobs</u> in support, and suppliers <u>for every job in the industry</u>. Not wise!

The next thing that you have to learn to fix is 'listening'. Your campaign minimized the biggest detriment to democracy by reforming campaign <u>fund raising</u>. By getting, on average, $100 from 10's of millions of ordinary people cuts out the big interest groups and lobbyists from <u>buying</u> the election. That's fine, but that is a two way street! When most of your money comes from a dozen lobbyists or big interests, you <u>know who to listen to and who to "pay back"</u>. When the bulk of your money comes from "the People of these United States" who do you listen to? Who's to Pay Back? The more important of these two is <u>who do you listen to</u>? Is it Move-on? Perhaps, but they really do not represent the views and feelings of the millions of people who contributed through them <u>out of pure convenience</u>. No, <u>you have to establish and foster contact points through out the US to tap what is going on locally</u> and to "pole" the feel or the tide of the interests on main street. <u>Health Care Reform is No. 1 Here!</u>

CHAPTER 8

<u>DAMNED</u>   Letter to the President 11/18/08

Holidays, Thanksgiving, it is time for being thankful for all of our bounteous abundance, the normal joyous time of year that most people look forward to enjoying - immensely. This is also the time of year when depression and suicides seem to be highest due to unrealized holiday expectations. Right now, this year about all that most people have to be thankful for is your joyous victory – and hopeful expectations for the future – <u>as yet unrealized and, unfortunately, not soon to be so!!</u>

I consider myself to be a part of the middle class. I made as much as $90,000 a year in my career and inherited a fair amount of money from my parents and in laws about 12 yrs. ago – most of which is now gone – not from spending it, but from the market damage and those wall street barons. I am lucky as a former middle class person to have a job when I need it at this time and at this time of year. I am extremely lucky as I have a good steady income from Social Security due to my moderate ten best earning years. Had Bush had his way, even that would be gone – perhaps not for me but others in a similar situation to myself. Without social security, the money I make at a full time job would not be near enough <u>by at least half</u> to keep us going. I can only keep going on a full time salary by virtue that I am old enough to collect Social Security - a situation that benefits only <u>a very few people facing these very hard times</u>. Can you imagine those 5 million+ people who are facing the collapse of the number one major employer of the nation, the auto industry – because they may be union members? - because the executives fly a private jet to DC to testify? - because their industry was forced to lose billions due to the financial crash and loss of credit caused by those totally irresponsible wall street rogues and the banking industries who were bailed out by the US taxpayers at a cost of almost a trillion dollars?! Twenty Five Billion – <u>a loan, not a gift or a bail out, but a loan</u> is chump change when compared to figures like a Trillion Dollars!!! Give us a break!! Give us <u>all</u> a break!!! After this election, it is hard to believe that it is politics as usual. It is unimaginable that one would even <u>take the time to argue</u> whether money would come from the $700 Billion or from a new bill! <u>Give us a break</u>. Like Nike, JUST DO IT!!

It is pure insanity as usual. You people are playing with people's <u>real lives</u> as being totally unimportant – totally irrelevant!! We are speaking of the very people who pay your salaries, and fill the coffers of the executives of this nation. They act as if we are chump change and of no consequence. You're not coming off well in this "game" - playing "your violin" at filling the cabinet <u>while Rome Burns</u>. I don't work for any car co., nor am I expecting to buy a car in the future - but I can tell you as sure as the nose on my face that my job, <u>will be grossly, adversely effected by this stupidity</u>. Standing at work I have many flash backs about all the <u>hard work and hard times that we went through to earn enough money to enjoy a retiremen</u>t only to see it all <u>go to hell</u> due to some very rich politicians and very rich opportunists who apparently <u>needed</u> our money more than we did. <u>Guess we're lucky they didn't need a lot more of it or it All Would Be Gone</u>!

CHAPTER 9

<u>DAMNED</u>　　　　　　　Letter to the President 11/23/08

I learned early in my corp. management experience that: - <u>Short Term Survival ALWAYS trumps long or mid range survival strategies</u>!! Said again - <u>Short Term Survival always trumps long or mid range survival strategies</u>!! It can't be emphasized strongly enough!! Forget about them being the Bad Boys – Just Do it!! Then we can worry about how to get them fixed to survive for the long term. They are not the bad dummies here, they are business people who know where their future lies. Besides, Paulsen just <u>gave</u> another 20 billion (after an initial $5 billion) to <u>bail out</u> Citi-Bank WITHOUT QUESTIONS ASKED. It's said they are carrying $300+ billion in toxic securities.

Besides, it seems it may be the oil industry that may have encouraged Detroit to make those gas guzzling cars and Hummers. Faced with the competition from the fuel efficient hybrids and the cost advantaged foreign companies, Detroit had to nail down a profitable niche that would and did compete with the foreign competition at a cost competitive disadvantage. It worked amazingly well as long as the price of oil did not rise too high. At $4.30-4.50 at the pump - conveniently in time for Bush to end the ban on off shore drilling just before the election - is when the S___ hit the fan for Detroit. Have you noticed that in just two months the price at the pump has dropped from $4.50 to $1.75 and to the best of my knowledge, there seemingly are no new refineries built, no new drilling, no new sources of oil and no sudden <u>lack</u> of Katrina's to blame for the decreases. Isn't that just special!! How convenient!! Yes, it was the financial market crash and the credit crunch that nailed the final dilemma for Detroit, not Detroit itself. People just could not buy them - not big ones and not even foreign ones like Toyota who is seemingly also in financial trouble.

Who benefits most from the financial BAIL OUT? You've got it - the richest, most irresponsible people in the world – not America. Who suffers the most from not LOANING this $25 Billion to the three Auto companies? Three to 10 million workers plus the support jobs, not to mention all of the rest of America that has already suffered in spades from Financial irresponsibility. If Detroit goes Chapter 11 and IF they do survive, A HUGE IF, it will be 3 million+ worker's salaries that pay the supreme price for the failure of others who should have known better and who collected huge bonuses and salaries the whole time. Obama, where is your commitment to those people of Michigan and Ohio during the campaign? Where is your mantra of change and a new way of doing things? Where is your humanity for the very people who probably got you elected? Keep playing your fiddle while Rome burns – and your administration will suffer. There are 8 more Fridays from now until Jan 20th. You can't bail out the economy with 8 more talks on radio!

I stated very clearly in my letter dated Oct 26, 2008 that you needed to establish a liaison office in the White House to fix the economy ASAP while giving Bush some legacy. See my quote on 10/26/08 - four weeks ago!: ""We have all the talent needed available now just sitting around being wasted at Starbucks etc."" (perhaps a metaphor, but not far from the truth). We need to get

24   these people back to work doing very productive work building our economy and future, but <u>the process needs to be jump started now</u> - almost immediately. Just after winning the election, you must insist on a liaison office in the White House to start the planning toward that goal. Now today, even Prominent ReCorpicons are chiding you to do just what I said you should do four weeks ago. They are begging you to do this now to get America at least partially back on track because <u>they know</u> that a totally irreversible disaster can happen in 8 weeks time without your direct involvement. <u>You have absolutely everything to gain by doing it, and absolutely EVERYTHING to lose by not doing it</u>.

You should establish a <u>Secretary of Technology</u> or at the very least a <u>Dept of The Future</u> for basic, emerging and strategic <u>technologies</u> and to help shape and promote necessary disciplines and identify areas for strategic federal funding to promote the interests of the Nation as well as Global strategic interests for World survival such as Global Warming. A national regional <u>Consultancy group on Products, Technologies and Industry</u> - experts who can advise you on strategic technological issues from a regional basis should be set up. A <u>Department of Peace</u> might be set up to change the role of minimalized people and nations who can and will cause global trauma if not attended to properly. All contribute to the general world economy and thus to stability and peace!

It's just <u>extremely hard to understand</u>, looking at this national crisis as we out here in America who are suffering from it materially and personally - and by those of the World who are looking at it with horror and a sense of complete and total disbelief, <u>why you</u> – our elected officials in congress and the government - seem to look at this calamity as if it <u>were a toy to be played with as by a cat or a dog</u>! You seem to deal with this crisis as if <u>you have</u> <u>your job</u>, <u>your salary</u>, <u>your future</u>, <u>your retirement</u>, <u>in the bag</u> so this might be just a distraction that can be dealt with in purely political terms - advantages, disadvantages, connections made, connections broken, <u>promises made</u>, <u>promises broken or never intended to be kept</u>, and in terms of purely self interest. That is <u>America as USUAL</u> this is <u>politics as USUAL</u> this is <u>old news</u> when you ran consistently on the hopeful message of <u>new News</u>. Your Presidency, as far as we are concerned, started on November 4 2008 – not 1/21/09.

To date, there has not been one "bail out" for those losing their jobs on a daily basis. There has not been one "bail out" for those losing their homes. There has not been one "bail out" for all the rest of us who have lost our <u>pensions, savings or retirement</u>. Your <u>plan</u> to create <u>2.5 million jobs</u> in two years <u>is CLEARLY NOT ENOUGH!</u> for the need that is immediate – we have lost a million jobs in just the past 10 months of this year alone. Meanwhile, Paulsen was given the keys to Ft Knox for <u>the biggest giveaway for the rich of all time</u>!! Where is the plan to <u>save those who have and are and will be paying for all of these and the other bail outs</u>? Have you forgotten who it is that really needs the bail out? Again, I don't mean just for people who have jobs or who are paying taxes!!!

<u>**IT MUST BE FOR EVERYONE!!!**</u>

CHAPTER 10

<u>DAMNED</u>　　　　　Letter to the President 11/25/08

On Monday you proposed to set up a WPA like (my 10/26/08 a month ago) job corps doing infrastructure work on bridges, roads, power grids, energy fields like wind farms, schools etc. - costing about 400 to 600 billion to create only <u>2.5 million jobs in 2 years</u>. By comparison we have lost over a million jobs in just the past 10 months and will <u>likely lose 0.25 – 3 million more before the inauguration</u>. These WPA like jobs are jobs that cannot be shipped overseas!! A whole new WPA process will be required. You should <u>KNOW this truth in 2-3 months</u>!!

Problem one: Not everyone is in construction or a road worker. There is neither time to retrain or an inclination on the part of most <u>out of work</u> to do road or construction work. Yes, there will be those who are or who can be trained, but that is probably only about 100,000 of the proposed 2.5 million. Excluding the supervision and engineers for these projects, most are blue collar jobs with blue collar hourly salaries. As a result <u>the tax base is minimal</u>. The second problem: Most local, state and national projects require a minimum of 6-12 months to plan and to obtain funding through government entities. Most require, lengthy feasibility and impact studies before that adding 1-1 1/2 more years before projects can start. <u>A whole new way is going to be required to implement this massive job creation in an ASAP way</u>.

I see that not only has Paulsen been given the 'keys to Fort Knox' to give to Wall Street but he has changed his mind and plans (without congressional approval) at least three times. Keep in mind, that his original proposal was a <u>three page bill</u> for congress. That was expanded to <u>535 pages</u>, under congressional intervention back in September. That CRISIS <u>JUST had to be solved then ASAP</u>, but most evidence seems to show that nothing has been done except to give the banks un-precedented amounts of money to little avail except to give them means to buy smaller banks <u>without actually solving the basics of the real monetary crisis facing America</u>.

<u>Main Street has not seen DIME ONE,</u> except to see trillions of their <u>yet unearned dollars disappear</u>. <u>Talk about building the proverbial trough and asking your piggy friends to belly up to the bar</u>. The first monetary rip off of the middle class was the contrived Iraq war. Now on the way out, they <u>appear</u> to have built the biggest extraction of all time without any restrictions, approvals or oversight and will be taking - without any approval what so ever - <u>all of the yet unearned monies</u> of our grand-children and great grand-children. Just a week ago, Paulsen said that he had done everything that was needed and would save $350 billion for the next administration. Today he says that he needs another $800 billion to put more food in the trough for those on Wall Street. Yet, there is no $25 billion <u>loan</u> to Detroit - main street – what a totally, unabashed, flamboyant, <u>hypocrisy</u>!!! This whole "financial crisis" is beginning to smell like yesterday's <u>bad fish left on the counter</u>. Actually it smelled bad the day it was bought – like smoke there is fire, it is beginning to <u>smell like</u> WE and YOU have been <u>had</u> yet one more time. ENOUGH!! I can't help but feel <u>they are laughing at US all the way to the bank or banks</u>!!! It has got to STOP!!

CHAPTER 11

<u>DAMNED</u>   Letter to the President 12/11/08

NERO (STILL) PLAYS WHILE ROME BURNS It is absolutely incredulous that in these unprecedented times of <u>staggeringly horrendous economic down turn</u>, job losses, foreclosures, recession stats and largest one month growth in unemployment – <u>that those who represent the people of the United States are STILL playing politics</u>. Has the Opposition Group learned absolutely nothing from this election? Have they learned absolutely nothing from the Gulf coast disasters? Rule one of Management 101 – <u>Short term survival always trumps long - mid range plans</u>.

We have lost 2.5 million jobs since the start of the year. <u>A 2.5 million job increase</u> in next two years <u>is just not going to do it</u>! If we lose our auto industries that increases it a minimum of 3 million more and with added ripple effects more like 10 million more! 2.5 million is but a ripple next to the 3 – 10 million if the auto industry goes down. Would you size this up as a time to "<u>play Chicken</u>"? I think NOT. <u>Well, some of our representatives seem to think so!!!</u>.

And where are you, president elect? Are you just playing "Chicken" as well? Are you letting the ReCorpicons hang themselves before you take office? Beware, a two bladed sword like that one <u>can cut both ways</u>! Actions, (<u>or lack therefrom</u>) can have consequences. A venture capitalist taught me a very valuable lesson a long time ago – Silence Lends (IS) Assent! That is and was a very profound and fundamental revelation. If one stays silent when something is "going down" they are "voting" for it by their silence just as loudly as if they had yelled "Yea".

What is <u>Even more powerful</u>, Forever more, they will <u>never</u> be able to stand up and say, "I told you so or I told you way back then that it was wrong, or Had you just listened to me, this would not have happened". No, <u>being silent is a very, very, very dangerous silence</u>!

One fundamental fact remains about the possibility of the auto industry's demise. You can speculate all you want – you can hypothesize all you want – you can predict all you want - you can pontificate all you want about <u>what will or will not happen</u> if they are not bailed out, but one thing is for sure – if they aren't bailed out Now <u>and they go down</u> – <u>no amount of pontificating is going to put them back together again!!</u> (Ref. Humpty Dumpty). In management 101 it's called the <u>Down Side vs Upside Evaluation</u>. It's a fundamental part of Risk Management or Risk Mitigation! For shame, you across the isle, you should, perhaps, know that far better than anyone else! What can they be thinking? Just go figure!!!

Are we as a nation really prepared to suffer the consequence if they go down beyond the direct financial consequences? Just paying the unemployment for those people is more than $15 Billion. Has anyone considered the tax loses from 10 million people? What about neighborhoods? Has anyone even thought of the impact on the simplest of needs and it's consequences on all of us? There are probably 100 million American made automobiles on the road. <u>Where in Hell are we going to get replacement parts for those vehicles for the next decade</u>? Where are we going to get our repairs? Has anyone thought about that? <u>That directly effects everyone</u>! It is truly time to Get Real!

CHAPTER 12

<u>DAMNED</u>   Letter to the President 12/25/08 - Xmas!

"It was the Best of times – It was the Worst of times" Charles Dickens. "Now is the Winter of our Discontent – Made Glorious Summer-" William Shakespeare. What did these two know then? How well did they <u>portend</u> their futures – or the<u> present times hundreds of years in the future</u>? Perhaps they <u>knew human nature so well</u> that their messages and word phrases were and are <u>timeless</u>!!

I see images of you on TV <u>basking and frolicking in the sun in Hawaii</u> while 2/3rds of <u>America is Suffering</u> - in many cases and places – <u>The Worst Winter in History</u>!! <u>Many</u> of us do not even know that it is Christmas except that it is on the calendar and there have been endless Holiday programs and Movies for a month on TV. <u>Yes, the worst Winter in History</u> not just because of the weather, <u>but for our bad times as well</u>! I have a huge limb that drove a 6 inch hole through the outer roof right over where my wife was sleeping - and <u>fortunately</u>, it didn't penetrate the inner ceiling. An hour later a 1.5 inch diameter branch shot through the roof and ceiling like a spear - jutting into the room 5 feet!! On the next day - Xmas Eave - a large tree fell across our yard and would have <u>smashed</u> our car – had I not ventured out 7:00 in the morning in a foot of snow – on un-plowed roads to open a store so that the owner - who sat at home watching the financial results on his computer - could <u>make a few more bucks</u> before year end and hopefully give us employees a small bonus – I do mean SMALL. And yet you are still basking in the sun for all to see!!

God knows you deserve it after that grueling campaign and time building your cabinet – and hopefully the rest and good times will rejuvenate you for the horrendous task before you – and for OUR America!!!

I have spoken many times since weeks before the election on Nov 4th that the job corps that must be rejuvenated is the highly technical job corps that has been laying dormant for these many years!! For each, single high tech job created, 100's to 1000's are generated in research and development groups, upper and middle management, plant managers and workers, architects and builders for new or to modify old sites.

To give a road worker or a bridge builder a job may provide perhaps 1 to 10 other mid to low paying jobs and then END!! And, how many of us out here are road or bridge builders? Damn few of us!! Your thinking and visions are too small, belittling, degrading for those of us 'virtually' unemployed in America. The tax revenues from high tech jobs are far greater than for low ones - not to mention the horrendous tax incomes from the sales and profits of these new businesses, resulting jobs and market structures. Real commerce would again be alive and providing large cash flows for Americans and America for a very long time -- versus those short term gains!!

Just for proof, I'll tell you about a recent article. A person needed 2-3 low level workers for a three week temporary situation. He advertised and was deluged with 100s of PhD's, high level scientists and managers responding to his low level temporary job. This is the story I am talking about here and now! Really needs attention!

32   Let me tell you also about three other things that have been noticed on TV recently. One is the Toxic Coal Slurry Dam that burst in Tennessee -flooding and wiping out hundreds of homes and miles of prime real estate and now is in danger of contaminating two major rivers and the drinking water of millions of the good people of Tennessee. Not saying this is a case, but <u>where there is smoke there is often fire</u> and this <u>smells like smoke.</u> Even if not related, it is a story that <u>reminds us</u> of the current administration's take on safety standards deregulation and relaxation for coal, chemical and other energy co.'s.

The 2nd story is about an add on CNN touting the benefits and importance of <u>human resources</u> organizations. I remember when human resources suddenly appeared in a very successful high tech company <u>that had done phenomenally well without their help for years before</u>. A large storage room across from my office was cleaned out and one person set up a desk there. Before three months had passed, the room contained some 10 people and they called themselves Human Resources. In all my years in industry, I have never seen such an example of hiring so many people for so little benefit & producing a <u>cost center</u> rather than a <u>Profit Center</u>. It was actually worse than a cost center as they became, instead, a <u>Reduction of Profit Center – or a basic liability</u>.

With that one person in that large storage room, I felt that I saw the start of the end for this successful start up company. These people have become an entity unto themselves - they also became a law unto themselves without real, meaningful oversight and almost no recourse provided to the employees.

Yes, I realize there are laws and regulations that need to be interpreted and applied, but believe me, in my opinion, it doesn't seem like a blessing to productive companies or organizations. They insert themselves between employees to be hired and the hiring manager – even to the extent of trying to re-interpret what the hiring manager actually meant when he said he wanted to hire someone. Decide for yourself. Enough about that.

The other media touted story is about those "out of work" Wall Street types wearing suits with signs saying "I Will do anything for work". Well <u>Sob Story</u>! It's about time. The only thing that should be done for that lot is require them to <u>pay back</u> last year's bonuses and fine them for having been so greedy and ruthless in helping to destroy our America. Jail would be too good for them – besides it would cost us too much money just to keep that lot in jail.

What talent do they have for sale? Who knows, con game management? Scam science? Excessive Greed Pedaling 101? Make it rich without training 202? Who knows? Perhaps, we should send them to Iraq and Afghanistan to clean up the mess over there. Let them get their jobs and real training under fire in those environments. It just might give them something to think about while trying to survive in that situation. Let them use their skills and cunning to rout out Osama bin Laden! Give me a break, they could live for years on just part of their salaries from one year or their golden parachutes. <u>Please do not forget those who actually voted for you as President – those of us struggling to pay YOUR SALARIES</u>

CHAPTER 13

<u>DAMNED</u>   Letter to the President 01/01/09 Cheers!

In these unprecedented times of staggering economic down turn, job losses, foreclosures and recession one thing may simply be overlooked in this overwhelming madness and that is the apparent loss of and possible reinstatement of <u>The Rule of Law</u>! This has suddenly been thrust into global importance with the action now going on in the Gaza Strip. <u>The Rule of Law is the very basis of and the very enabler of Democracy</u>! Without <u>honoring</u> the Rule of Law, Democracy would have been essentially suspended and without taking <u>real action</u> to <u>correct</u> those suspensions it is doubtful that it can exist.

What we may have lost may not even be known and yet to heal the Democracy that we all so much espouse to and desire, we truly need to do what we can to not only reestablish the Rule of Law, we need to Examine the part that seems absent from us. That means a thorough examination of everything that may have transpired. The constitution <u>is at risk</u> & requires that we do what we can to bring what may have been to light. Otherwise, moving to the future <u>without restoring that part of Democracy</u> that has been suspended –just simply becomes a sham.

With all of the activity of selecting and naming your cabinet, please do not forget your number one asset – Joe Biden. He is the one stable, sage wisdom that you will need to count on to temper the hotly blowing winds of that extremely diverse cabinet. You will need that steady, measured, practiced, timeless, historic insight and perspective brought by Joe Biden in brisk, hot times!

You know better than I that a tax cut IS NO SOLUTION TO TURN AROUND A BAD ECONOMY IN SHORT TERM!! At best, a tax cut will save a few bucks each pay day from now till nowhere. At worst, it will not put money into the pockets of those most in need of that money today - not until long past when it is needed – not until June of 2010!! We desperately need this money now – TODAY! To do this with a tax cut make the Tax cut retroactive to 2008 so that filing in a month or two, the $500 or $1,000 will come back to us as a refund in February through June this year. Those who don't need to pay taxes, will simply file a 1040EZ to get the $1000 even if they did not make enough to file otherwise. Of course, those whose FAGI is more than, say, $80,000 will not be eligible for this refund.

Apparently, those who represent the people of the United States are STILL playing politics. Did they learn nothing from this election? Did they learn nothing from the Gulf coast disasters? Rule one of Management 101 – Short term survival always trumps long or mid range planning.

We have lost 2 million jobs in the last qtr of the year. A 3.0 million job increase over the next two years is just not going to cut it! It is not a time to "play Chicken"! We need to kick start high tech and high level jobs to turn around not only the economy, but to prime the pump to pay back the huge deficit. These high technological jobs will create companies that will hire 100's to 1000's of employees at all levels and in green energies that cannot be exported to Asia. Take a $150 billion of the Tarp to create a venture capital fund to start these new companies. Take $100 Billion to pay for high Technology education scholarships to supply the new tech industries.

CHAPTER 14

DAMNED   Letter to the President 2/09/09

Oh, I am very sorry. You became president on 1/20/09 as the world <u>clambered</u> with <u>celebration</u>, horrendous joyous relief, <u>jubilation</u>, gigantic crowds, a flood of sudden relief as if just let out of a life sentence in Abu Ghraib Prison with a reprieve contrived by <u>the people themselves</u> suddenly released from a VERY LONG 8 year sentence. With just such a <u>glorious prologue</u> <u>you had to run into the most intolerable</u>, <u>business as usual</u>, deliberate trouble making partisanship - seemingly geared only to make you not only look like a fool but to destroy whatever mandate that you had so deservedly earned and had intended to spend. Is there no honor among thieves?!!

Did they learn <u>nothing</u> from this election? Did they learn nothing from the past 8 years? Did they learn what 300 million people of the USA and the entire rest of the world wanted to happen after this <u>frozen winter of discontent during the past 8 years</u>? We cannot tolerate this radical crowd of nay sayers destroying what we the People of these United States mandated you to do. <u>You won the election</u>. You are the President of the United States – not John McCain. Both Democrats <u>and ReCorpicons</u> are truly seeing the true colors that were there all along in the race but now the Wolf in Sheep's clothing is exposed!

The American public is so fed up with those who are seemingly appearing to be obstructionists. Forget the 60 votes, you only need 51 in the Senate to pass – let them filibuster again and again over the weekend, all day and all night for a week if you have to – have TV cover them and let them make fools of themselves. What happened to the Nuclear Option that put the US in panic when they wanted us to vote for Judges etc.? Where is the guts? Where is the backbone? Where is the Honor?

They have just got to learn, that after these past 8 years of voting in the Bushes, squandering a 4 Trillion dollar surplus making it a 4 trillion dollar deficit in just 8 years that they have no Moral Authority whatsoever - High, Middle or Low - to do anything but sit down, clasp their hands, and vote yea for what ever comes across their desk. They blew it so big time that it hurled chunks! Yuck!

And John McCain!!! Boy has he shown his true colors!!!! He seems no more a change artist than the Bushes that he grew up in. Some Maverick he turned out to be – Party Line, Party Line all the way Oh, just like, what did I say? on 10/04/08 a third year ago! It suddenly occurred to me there are only two things that consistently characterized the ReCorpicon Group over the past two decades. In a word: the Party of NO!! And the Party of Obfuscation. They consistently seem to do everything in their power to say NO to everything America needs and wants to do including controlling our very lives at home in a very negative way. They have developed the strategies and methods of Obfuscation to an art by trivializing science and experience to Stop everything that is needed by people and government whether they are in power or OUT. No matter the issue or it's validity, create 1-10 other "fictitious options" and present them as if valid to totally confuse and destroy valid action. Note this on Global Warming, Stem Cells, Evolution, Right to Life, Health Care!

CHAPTER 15

<u>**DAMNED**</u>   Letter to the President 2/28/09

Oh, what a glorious "State of the Union" Address!! I would not have wanted to be the opposition trying to make a rebuttal after that hopeful and all encompassing message! You said it all and left absolutely nothing for them to say, counter or do that you had not thoroughly covered. Anything they said after that would not only completely alienate 90% of America, but would also further make them look foolish. Poor Bobby Jendal, after your speech, I'd said, "I'm sorry, I'm just not doing this."

Do you know what your recovery plan and budget has that invites attack? <u>They're called budgets</u>. Budgets and plans are for a Nation at peace and prosperous! We are a <u>Nation at WAR</u>! We are in the midst of a "war" on the Nation's Depression. <u>Make no mistake about it, this is no less a war than a war on Terror or in Iraq or Afghanistan</u>. This is <u>worse than the worst war this nation has ever faced</u> - our very <u>existence as a nation hangs in the balance</u>!! THIS IS WAR AND WAR REQUIRES <u>WAR MEASSURES</u> AND <u>WARTIME EXPENDITURES</u> and DEMANDS THAT YOU BE THE COMMANDER IN CHIEF to <u>execute it</u> SUCCESSFULLY!!

I don't know why it's called a Depression - this is more like a 1000 Katrina's or a 100 911's!! We find our enemy is within! Did we fight the war in Iraq/Afghanistan without spending trillions of dollars? NO!!!! Did we fight WWII or the Korean War without huge extraordinary amounts of money? Hell No!! So how is this war any less important than these? Did the "Group of Conscience" stop to challenge the extraordinary expenditures for those wars in the past 8 years? Absolutely Not! Did anyone in congress not support the troops in these wars? No they always supported the troops as being patriotic.

Where is their patriotism when the "troops" are those fighting it out on main street America in the very war that is killing the very foundation of this nation and its very right to exist? Are these troops any less deserving of their support than those in foreign lands? NO!! Are their circumstances and plight any less dire than those valiant warriors in far off places? Hell NO!! Make no mistake, this is war, this is THE war to end all wars and we cannot SURVIVE if we LOSE THIS ONE! We are given only one good battle, one good fight and only one plan! As in war, there can be only one plan and it's your plan as President of the United States - the Commander in Chief!!

When we were growing up during those prosperous times in America when we were building the new electronic industrial complex, new products, the future, in companies like IBM, DuPont, Hewlett Packard, Tektronix, TI, Motorola, GE and 3M, we received Xmas "letters" from our friends and former classmates that bragged about how successful their children were and how well they were doing in their careers. We used to laugh at how much they seemed to exaggerate, but looking back they were not all that inaccurate. Today, all we see are Xmas "letters" about holes in the roof from severe storms, loss of retirement, getting a part time job to make ends meet, a severe illness that threatens to ruin what is left. The high tech want adds used to cover 4-5 pages -now if they exist at all they cover only a corner of one page!!!

CHAPTER 16

<u>DAMNED</u>   Letter to the President (3/09/09)

Big home run on stem cell research. We have lost way too many valuable years of initiative to others in other countries. We must take back the lead and recapture the 100's of billions of dollars in potential products, industry and lucrative opportunities in patents and companies! They need to sense the reality of the real world and get on board. This seems just one of those manufactured issues to obfuscate what needs to be done. No more, no less. Also give it a home run on separation of science from politics or religion or the use of science for political or religious ends. Right on - back to reality.

I also notice from the Science Magazine that your plan to stimulate the economy gives money to NASA, NSF and other groups that would be involved in high level research and development. Right on, this is essential to re-build the middle class and stimulate the high end research for products and companies. This, as a part, can be quite significant for a quick national recovery.

It would sure be a great help if we saw less of Robert Gibbs. He seriously needs to improve in his style and delivery. Hopefully, much progress will be made soon.

What if McCain had been elected to this mess, what do you think he would have done? It is clear that <u>he would have had to do a lot more than just tax cuts</u> if he thought he might make a difference in the end. Though, a little different in some minor aspects, it likely would have been very much similar to what you are doing and proposing. With a stacked house and Senate against him, do you think that the Democrats would have been called obstructionists? Do you think that they would have fought his plan tooth and nail? The shoe very much could have been on the other foot and they would be playing out in the field of frustration! It's something to think about when they are so quick to criticize and block movements to solve the problems we are ALL facing – including the opposition, the hard core friends, their minor constituents.

On the hold over budget, just tell them that if they are so against voting for the bill because of the ear marks, that you'll gladly take out the ear marks of those opposing the bill. Then it is fair for all again. They seem so proud of their "necessary" ear marks that they just have to stay in the bill! What Hypocrites!! They seem to be running so hard in every direction but the one that is needed to get the job done to save this nation that they appear to be a confused lot "just saying NO to everything that's right".

It finally seems clear to me what the real difference is in the two camps. The Opposition stands on "principle or principles" – <u>simple catch phrases</u> to be focused on and retained as a "mantra" such as "Less Taxes, No Taxes, Less Government, Right to Life, States Rights, Business knows best, Etc.". Then they spend all their time/energy developing rationalizations, arguments, strategies and campaigns <u>to sell</u> these simple constructs. Progressives <u>see problems</u> and <u>work to solve</u> them using pragmatism, logic/science & talking. However, there is not just one solution or one <u>simple catch phrase</u> that works so they appear confused or divided when the <u>opposite is true</u>!!

CHAPTER 17

<u>DAMNED</u>   Letter to the President (6/19/09)

Just a back up note! Solving complex problems requires a great deal of discussion, negotiations, investigations, data, facts, review of past programs and performances, listening to the various professional disciplines that have real knowledge of the mechanisms of the problems and working together to find <u>a or the</u> most pragmatic answer. This is <u>almost never</u> embodied in a <u>simple catch phrase</u>! Dumbing down science and education is a <u>means to an end</u> not a practical way to deal with complex problems!

Well, a lot of water has gone under the bridge and is now time to try to find a wrap up of the results of the first <u>150 days</u> of a <u>1460 day</u> administration period - about 10%!!

What was restated in par 1, 2 Chap. 11 on what to do with Detroit was ignored. These are the people that perhaps helped get you elected. We're talking perhaps a 30 billion dollar LOAN to the one <u>major REAL manufacturing industry</u> left in American <u>responsible for one out of every ten jobs in America</u>. These are <u>not the people</u> who bankrupted America, the world, and all of our bank accounts and in particular all of our RETIREMENTS!!! NO, that bunch all got hundreds of billions in GIFT bail out monies and paid out millions of dollars in bonuses to the very people responsible for bankrupting all the rest of us. <u>This leaves a long malingering taste we will never forget</u>!!

<u>Rule Number Two of Business</u>!! <u>Never</u> Fire your Sales Force when your business is down from a drop in Sales. And yet Chrysler is closing ~ 900 of its sales units and GM is

closing ~ 1200 of theirs. Is this job creation? What are they going to do – start selling all of the competitor's cars? Boy, that really sounds like good business sense!!

And now it is apparent that there may be a possible, but yet <u>fully unintended</u> consequence of this almost sure run to bankruptcy of these two Giants of our manufacturing. Having been "forced" to choose bankruptcy vs. keeping going temporarily with a small loan, these car companies are very likely to reorganize to the extent of going totally offshore to do their manufacturing. <u>Well, isn't that just special!</u>!! That sure keeps 100's of thousands of our hard working people hard at it in the rust belt of America!! 30 Billion is a drop in the bucket of the bail outs and little to pay to maintain 1/10 of our entire work force. It was the auto industry that turned on a dime in WWII to build our planes, tanks and armaments. Where will we turn to if needed in the future? <u>We can't survive as a service industry country or as a financial rip off country</u>!!!

It sure is good to see that congress has taken on the credit card companies. That is a good start and most of the provisions that needed to be fixed seem to be fixed. However, as mentioned before, the real culprit that must be addressed is the banks themselves. They have the same if not more insidious practices to make 1/3 of their entire profits or about 33 Billion Dollars – intentionally created over-draft fees. This has got to be fixed next.

It's interesting how these companies cry out that this legislation would raise the cost of services!! It sounds like a bank robber complaining when finally caught after getting by committing robberies for years - Scott Free!!

44	There's the <u>primary</u> goal to create a <u>single payer health care</u> or at least a <u>public option health care bill</u> that <u>fixes a host of EVILS</u> that currently exist in our health delivery industry!! An extremely high priority includes a total revamping or re-writing of the Part D drug bill for Senior citizens. Part D is the greatest abomination of all time! Clearly, it was written by health care, drug and pharmaceutical companies and their lobbyists!!

OBFUSCATION IS NOT ONLY A STATEGY BUT A TACTIC USED BY THE OPPOSITION TO STOP THE HEALTH CARE REFORM THAT <u>WE ALL ELECTED YOU TO GET PASSED</u> AS SOON AS YOU CAN AND GET SIGNED INTO LAW!! <u>WE CANNOT WAIT A DAY LONGER, A WEEK LONGER OR EVER.</u>

<u>THIS IS EXTREMELY IMPORTANT NOT TO BE FORGOTTEN!!!</u>

You, and those Legislators <u>were elected on your coat tails by the large majority of the citizens of these United States for ONE REASON AND ONE REASON ONLY</u> – TO PASS A <u>SWEEPING</u> HEALTH CARE BILL that solves many things. <u>YOU WERE NOT ELECTED BY DRUG, HEALTH CARE OR INSURANCE COMPANIES!! THEY HAVE NO SAY IN THE OUTCOME!! ELECTIONS HAVE CONSEQUENCES!!</u> It must contain a <u>PUBLIC OPTION. There can be no wavering on this!! This is an ABSOLUTE</u> – "It must be THERE or there is no CARE". It must eliminate – PRE EXISTING CONDITIONS!!! IT MUST INCLUDE TOTAL TRANSFERABILITY FROM ONE PLAN TO ANOTHER AND ONE COMPANY TO ANOTHER WITHOUT ANY PENALTY OR DETRIMENT WHAT-SO-EVER. IT MUST ELIMINATE OR GREATLY REDUCE THE DOUGHNUT HOLE IN PART D. IT MUST REDUCE HEALTH CARE COSTS FOR ALL.

CHAPTER 18

<u>DAMNED</u>   Letter to the President (7/19/09)

READ MY LIPS!!!!!!!! – <u>YOU WERE ELECTED</u> BASED ON YOUR GETTING A PUBLIC HEALTH PLAN <u>PASSED</u> AND THERE IS NO TIME TO WASTE!! IT MUST BE DONE AND DONE NOW!!!!!!! WE HAVE WAITED FOR DECADES AND WE CAN'T WAIT ANOTHER MINUTE! Forget the Opposition – No credibility!!!

<u>We gave you a super majority in the House and a 60 vote majority in the Senate to get this and other things done - there are absolutely no excuses, no alternatives ifs ands or buts about this</u> – it has absolutely got to be done and your number one priority. It is <u>time to prove to us</u> that you truly meant what you said that it is <u>time for a change</u> – a complete change that all of us out here and those with Move-On believed in enough <u>to fund your election and to get you and all those other SERVANTS OF WE THE PEOPLE ELECTED</u>!!! Those who voted for you voted for you for just one reason and it was a universal or/a public health care option. This is not <u>and I repeat</u> – MUST NOT BE a BIG BUSN., INSURANCE CO., OR A CORPORATE OPTION. <u>This is Gov. By and For the People not Corps.</u> Your legacy totally depends upon this being successful!! We are truly serious about this – there is no turning back now!!!! No Faint of Heart, no Oh well, perhaps next time – <u>NOW IS THE ONLY TIME TO DO IT - MAKE IT STICK</u>!!!!

That other bunch tries to claim we have the best health care in the world. That is pure Bull Shit! We have the most expensive Health care, the least effective Health care, the least efficient Health care, the most profitable for Corps Health care in the world. When compared to 30

46 other countries, we rank about 26. Bull Shit! It has got to change and change NOW!!!!!!! When people can go to foreign countries and get better care and operations so cheap that it pays for the travel costs – that says there is something definitely very, very wrong with our system!!

Forget about all those "so called huge Deficits". We weren't responsible!! They took a $4 Trillion surplus to a $4 Trillion Deficit in just 8 years. We are so jaded by those huge numbers now that we frankly just don't care anymore. However, we do care about the Huge loss of Jobs, the Huge loss of Homes, the Huge reductions in Salaries, The Huge loss of all of our Retirements and our continued loss of Cost Cutting HEALTH Care Options!!

Your Stimulus plan, (actually it was the Bush plan) seems to have helped the Banks, Wall Street and the Insurance companies very, very well. Huge profits just 6 months after Billions were poured into their coffers. Where are the Billions poured into Main Street – the ones who truly are the ones suffering and very badly! After all, it was those same Banks, Wall Street and Ins. Companies that not only bankrupted the US, it's people, but the Rest of the World as well. We will not forget that they are still the ones getting huge salaries and huge bonuses while we are losing our jobs, our homes, our raises, our salaries, our retirements, our well being, our happiness and sense of doing well and our wellness!! We are truly getting very PISSED OUT HERE SEEING WHAT WE SEE IS HAPPENING AND IT DOES NOT PLEASE US IN THE VERY LEAST. Enough Said!!

There is a case on trial out in Oregon that is interesting if one only thinks about the implications in the right way.   If

examined it has real import for present health care! 47
A religious couple is being tried for <u>murder</u> of their child that died from a curable disease <u>as a result of their not believing in using doctors to treat their child</u>.

If they can be tried for murder, then why are our present insurance companies not <u>on Trial for Murder</u> when they get between the Doctor and Patient and <u>prevent the one action</u> that <u>everyone knows</u> is the <u>one thing that must be done to save a child or a person from death</u>. This seems no less like Murder than a couple believing they had the solution to the illness by their religion, and the child dies.

Those 900 people a week – <u>people who are dying</u> as a result of not getting the <u>care indicated and prescribed by their Doctors</u> – directly as the result of actions that their insurance companies took simply to maximize profits, pay exorbitant salaries, bonuses and pay for huge advertising budgets. **<u>THEY ARE KILLING PEOPLE FOR PROFIT</u>**!!! This is like the worst possible kind of murder – A MURDER BASED purely ON A PROFIT MOTIVE – like an armed robbery gone bad!! The most <u>heinous</u> of CRIMES!! THEY ARE TRADING LIVES FOR MONEY – LOTS OF MONEY!!!

<u>Present a health care plan</u> that will double or triple in cost in ten years – will bankrupt companies and thus the nation not to mention all those that must pay for it and <u>you would not get one congressman to vote for it</u> – not even the conservatives!! <u>Guess what?</u> That <u>IS THE PLAN we all have now – unworkable – unaffordable – BROKEN</u>!!

Take a look at Part D, now there is a total abomination. The only thing that they did right - you could take a long hard lesson - is that they planned and <u>wrote that one out</u>

48 long in advance and rammed it down the throats of congress even though there was a fair amount of opposition even on their side's part! To some, it was thought to cost too much and they even lied about that so that they could get it passed. I remember that vote and the problems they had. That is the only thing they did right, the rest is a total abomination.

The worst part – among its many, many, many horrible obviously horrible features – is the horrible feature that is so subtle that most people are not even aware of it yet – though they will be finding out soon enough. The Deductible goes up every year, the initial coverage reduces every year and the donut hole gets larger every year. Think about it. If all those things change as little as 5% a year, there will essentially be zero coverage by the time you would be old enough to retire and be eligible for coverage. Now that is a great plan!!! I realize that neither you nor those in congress will ever have to worry about that, but the facts remain for the rest of the country – it becomes essentially useless in about 20 years. Part D has got to be fixed or scrapped or converted over to a universal health plan as part of the new health plan or at least part of a public option. A visa versa may work also.

There is no reason why everyone in America cannot have as good a plan as Congress – NOW – especially since we the public are the ones paying all of their handsome salaries and Retirements. Since we are paying their salaries, and they are there to serve us, then we should get as good as what we have provided for them!!

CHAPTER 19

<u>DAMNED</u>　　　　　　　Letter to the President (8/29/09)

THIS IS IT!! Without a sweeping health care reform with a <u>sound, public option</u> in Congress -signed this year, we all have very little left to live for. Without passing the things you <u>promised and we all voted for you for</u>, there just is no hope left!!, Certainly, there is no more audacity of hope. And then, as Kennedy would say – <u>THE DREAM IS DEAD!</u>

This bill must be called the "Kennedy Better Health Care Bill! This is truly what 60+ % of Americans want and voted <u>you and all of those congressmen from red states in to do</u>. <u>To do less</u> is not only a <u>horrendous travesty against the entire American Public</u> – ironically, also against those <u>few</u> seemingly misinformed souls who are <u>irrational</u> and <u>shouting</u> about this issue – but to the future of the Entire Nation, its prosperity, its soundness of business, its very essence as a Democracy, its reputation and, on the whole, in each and every aspect that it operates and in which it can be felt and measured! <u>We will all die from it</u>!!

<u>We were not slackers</u>, dead beats or lazy clouts!! We all worked very hard all of our lives - saving what we could – some with advanced degrees in very hard subjects!!! We <u>now feel</u> we may have been duped - working all those years <u>in vain</u> only to see what futures and meager fortunes that we may have accumulated – <u>obliterated</u> by the past decade of <u>taking it from the poor and giving it to the rich</u>! <u>We have had enough and are in no mood for COMPROMISE of any kind what-so-ever</u>!!! Wall Street and Fast Business-as-usual got theirs. <u>ITS CLEARLY OUR TURN</u>!! <u>We are the ones paying for it, therefore it is & will be ours</u>!

50
DAMNED

CHAPTER 20
Letter to the President (9/19/09)

A PROMISE IS A PROMISE!

IT'S JUST NOT CARE – IF IT'S NOT THERE!!

A CONTRACT IS A CONTRACT!

An offer was made by your campaign for a <u>Strong Public Health Care Option</u>. The contract was signed by WE THE PEOPLE when we ensured your election and a strong majority in the House and a Filibuster proof majority in the Senate <u>swept in on your coat-tails to do just that – pass a Strong Public Option Health Care Bill</u>! Now, by the terms of that contract, <u>it is time to deliver</u> on the <u>Strong Public Health Care Option</u> -- Not a co-op or a bill greatly watered down by the Corps. & opposition in committee.

IF IT'S NOT THERE, THERE IS NO CARE!!!!

<u>That Senate bill just introduced is totally unacceptable and is a Total Joke</u>. After spending all that "Bi-Partisan" time working out detail after detail with the opposition getting giant <u>corporate favoring compromises</u> into the bill, <u>they wouldn't even stand with the committee chairman</u> when the bill was introduced. <u>Well, I hope he got His because We sure didn't get Ours</u>!! Why bother having them cooperate if they get all they want and will still not vote for it. That's a win – win for them and a lose – lose for us. Better, just pass what WE THE PEOPLE <u>NEED</u> and WANT instead. These sentiments come to mind: <u>Here We (I) Sit all Broken-Hearted, We (I) Paid our Quarter and THEY (He) only FA TED</u>.   NICHT WAR?!!

CHAPTER 21

DAMNED — Letter to the President (11/4/09)

Well, it's been a year since that Glorious, Jubilant, Highly Anticipated evening. A year later, <u>We are Not Enjoying</u> the victory as <u>we knew we would</u> on the night the people of the USA were <u>totally</u> responsible for your election!! I so remember you and Michelle Rock'n and Roll'n when the "GET A LIFE" band passed your stand late in the parade!

I hope you are saying a <u>Hell of a Lot More</u> privately to the congress than you are to the rest of us because, you are just not coming across as engaged in getting THE MOST IMPORTANT LEGISTRATION of the <u>century</u> passed <u>in a form that WE the PEOPLE need it to be passed</u>. <u>Ten pages</u> is all that is needed to fix a <u>Medicare E</u> for all that need it !! We <u>have</u> to have something simple like that <u>without the crap</u>!

Those people in DC seem to think that they <u>can just play around</u> with our <u>lives</u> as if <u>we really don't exist or simply don't matter</u>!!! Well, <u>we do matter</u>, that is why it is called Government By and For the People. <u>We are the people</u>!! See Par. 2, page 19, as to <u>who to listen to and pay back</u>!!!

Why are Gaithner and Summers on your Financial Team? With Greenspan they were <u>architects of this horrendous financial collapse in the US and the World</u>. They were for complete deregulation that allowed the dangerous, dubious, OTC derivatives market to exist, thrive and expand to the point of collapse of the world market. They beat down Brooksley Born who tried to regulate these markets and warned of this current catastrophe. This doesn't smack of a change for <u>We the People</u>!! You have much to answer for and we are the <u>ones to answer</u>!

CHAPTER 22

<u>DAMNED</u>   Letter to the President (11/22/09)

Well, well, well, finally a bill on the floor in the Senate! I don't have to tell you, I'm sure, that no matter what they <u>do</u> in the House and Senate with a Health Care reform bill <u>you only will be blamed</u>. It will not reflect upon them, it will reflect ONLY ON YOU, MR. PRESIDENT!! If the health care bill with the public option that more than 65% of the Americans sent you to the White House to get passed for them doesn't get passed by both houses and sent to you to sign, you will be the only one remembered negatively.

How can this happen? How can our representatives ignore what we need and want and must have? How, can the Democrats who were sent by those same 65% of Americans to pass this bill for them even consider not voting for it. IT WILL DO THEM ALL HARM AS WELL AS THE DEMOCRATIC GROUP FOR MANY, MANY YEARS TO COME.

Let's examine the motives of the opposition. They'll not pass <u>anything that you or we want</u>. There can be no compromise to be made with them or their business and corporate sponsors & cronies. It is clear that the United States of the Founders is not the United States of Today. They envisioned a government <u>by and for the people</u> where – despite differences of style, philosophy or process – our representatives would get together and try to solve the pertinent issues of their time to serve – guess who – WE THE PEOPLE OF THESE UNITED STATES!! That didn't involve solving the perceived needs of corporate or business America first. Apparently now, <u>neither side</u> has any perceived need to solve <u>America's real problems</u>.

CHAPTER 23   DAMNED   Letter to the President (12/25/09)

Do you know the <u>JUDAS GOAT</u>? I'M SURE YOU DO!! Most of us feel like we followed and supported a Judas Goat, got him elected and then were led <u>right into</u> the Corp. <u>slaughtering pens</u> of the Opposition, the ReCorpiCons the Insurance Co.'s the Pharmaceutical Co.'s, Wall Street and the Financial Hustlers. Well, it's a <u>horrible</u> feeling and there's just a hell of a lot of us here who feel down right <u>cheated and betrayed</u>. Remember chap. 7, Pg 19 where I talked about who you needed to pay back? It's US, yes, it's US – <u>We the People of these United States</u> – clearly not Wall Street, not the huge corps, not the Drug companies, not the Insurance co's and not the Financial Gurus. With our hard fought and <u>harder to give up</u> $50 and $100's we bought and paid for your election and we certainly deserve better, FAR BETTER than WHAT WE HAVE GOTTEN.

<u>First of all, get rid of the Goldman Sachs and Financial connections on your team</u>, Take a very strong stand on cleaning out the lobbyists and their influence. <u>Have the congress pass a 10 page Medicare E bill for all of those who cannot afford health insurance</u>, ban the use of prior conditions and rate hikes and end caps on annual and lifetime coverage. I'm afraid, that this congress, particularly the Democrats, have shown the entire world what a <u>total sham</u> this kind of a Democracy really is!!! I'm totally stressed to have been a part of or associated with this Party & government this past six months. Hell, clearly anyone with an ounce of good sense could have done far better. Go Figure!

54   Certain ones who shall be nameless are total A__ holes – neo Hit___s as far as we are concerned – and do not deserve a day longer in the office they now reside. Lynden Johnson would have ripped that bunch a new exit hole and certainly would not have allowed them to succeed. It is a total sham and unmitigated farce of the highest and lowest orders - simultaneously!!!

I swear, if a dozen astronomers found a huge meteorite heading for the world – scheduled to collide and destroy all of earth in 5 years - that this opposition would first deny that it even exists and then would do everything in their power to oppose and defeat anything and everything that the Admin set out to mitigate that certain catastrophe. Then as a last resort, they would propose a TAX CUT to fix it!!! This is the result of IGNORANT DESIGN -- they would cut off all lives just for spite. This parallel to the Global Warming debate is so close that it is Damn Scary!!

Jesus taught love and compassion for one's enemies as well as their friends. He taught tolerance of all types and styles and caring for those who are less fortunate than themselves. This ReCorpiCon Group seems to be hell bent on only promoting segregation between themselves and all others, condemning all of those who do not believe like them, propagating wars where wars are not needed and trying to collect as much of the world's wealth in the shortest possible time at the extreme detriment of all others who used to enjoy some comfort of a good job and a decent salary with benefits. There just seems to be no dealing with this kind of Taliban or Al Quaida. Nicht War? It so much sounds like Rome in the 3rd century just before the final conclusion and end.

CHAPTER 24 — Letter to the President (1/11/10)
DAMNED

To Joe Biden: I/we, all want to convey our deepest, most heartfelt condolences on the passing of your mother. My father died when he was 92 by a similar set of circumstances and we were all very saddened by his passing and welcomed any comfort that was extended to us. We are hoping that you are being showered with much love and caring in your family's time of grief.

I've neglected throughout the writing of this diary to talk about the "<u>macro</u>" <u>picture</u> that you, Joe, have lived through as well and by now must recognize as a root cause to what we are seeing in <u>all of America</u> and <u>in particular in Congress</u> that has led directly to all of <u>our destructions and frustrations</u>. The present crisis of our government and congress is the "epiphany" providing the "AH HA" moment that <u>shines so much brilliant light on the many ills and maladies of these following scenarios</u>.

We grew up in the 40's–80's when companies, both large and small, were started, built and thrived <u>spectacularly</u> on the simple principle of providing a <u>product of high quality</u> that is needed, wanted and sought after by their customers. Competition to <u>provide more or better</u> was between companies such as a Tektronix and a Hewlet Packard. At least 2 times a year they introduced better products at trade shows in NY and SF. The time between was spent in designing and manufacturing the <u>latest and greatest</u> new products - <u>all just to attract new customers</u>!!

We have experienced since then a <u>horrible shift</u> to a business model of "growing so large", so secure or so

56   aloof that instead of "serving" customers, they have devised and put in place models to rip off the customers they have who are totally at their mercy. Some services like banking, insurance, pharmaceuticals and energy have become so "necessary" and indispensible that the customers, in effect, either have no options or just ones that require paying a huge penalty of some kind that is dictated by that company or industry. Much of the American business model has shifted from products that serve to "service" that TAKES. With products, wealth is generated by adding value to materials through labor. Service takes money from entities that require the service - generally without adding value. Value comes from the customers. Because they have become so indispensible, they can literally make up new fees, administer and alter agreements at will with no recourse for the customer and with total impunity, lack of regulation or penalty at all.

We all remember when Ma Bell was a monopoly!! Perhaps you remember a cartoon, possibly in the New Yorker, where the Ma Bell employee said to the customer, "Well, you could always go to our competitor". After that, Ma Bell was split up into a lot of Mini Ma Bell's that also seem to have the same attitude, though somewhat diluted by a form of competition. Now we are all besieged by "offers to" buy into a service at a reduced rate for a year if you will only agree to sign a two or three year contract with them. Have you noticed that most product prices tend to come down with time as volume or improvements in manufacturing are passed on to customers? Cable companies, a service business, seems to raise prices every year even though by now, their "networks" are well established and their base of operations are pared down to the bone. They seem to constantly raise prices because they can with impunity!!

Our recent and very near recent demises from Wall St., insurance and the energy giants point to basic flaws in this Business Model itself and in particular in the lack of meaningful regulation and oversight for these businesses.

We cannot drive something as simple as a car without a whole book of laws and regulations. We cannot drive a car for long if we don't "inspect" them and fix their ailments. The most meaningful service is forward looking "preventative" exams that identify problems before they become catastrophic. That's just simple logic is it not true? The same is true for flying an airplane or running an airline. The regulation book is HUGE compared to cars.

If the concept and simple logic of necessary regulation is so obvious and well accepted for cars then why do some people claim it is possible to run huge, complex financial institutions without regulations, thorough inspections or total transparency? That thinking is not just ludicrous – it is completely insane and totally dangerous!! Those who claim that all businesses run far better if simply left alone are not only deliberately lying, if truly believed, they are totally dangerous hypocrites and should be censured.

The most dangerous part of this business model is that these "indispensible", not value creating, but revenue collecting service companies become so large that they "cannot fail" lest they endanger the financial health of the entire nation – and in this case the entire world. Then they can demand to be bailed out by governments even though they are the ones who have created the financial demise and catastrophe. They take our money and turn around and pay themselves first and still do not provide a real service to those who they claim to be their customers and who quite begrudgingly bailed them out and kept them from failing from the result of their greed and high risk practices performed without oversight or regulation. This alone is bad enough, but they add insult to injury by paying huge sums of our money to pay lobbyists to "buy off" congressmen to do their bidding instead of their "well defined job description" of the Congress to Serve We the People of These United States!!

Nowhere has this been more exposed than in the debate to try to enact a health care reform bill in the House and the Senate!! We have quite amply seen the worst of the worst outcomes of the consequences of these huge, powerful corporate and industry interests dictating to OUR PUBLIC REPRESENTATIVES to NOT DO the PEOPLE'S BIDDING!!! We should be outraged!! We should be protesting in the streets!! We should be hanging in effigy, but we are not doing it!!! We are not, apparently, because these interests have so pervaded our "culture" that we are content to partake of the "Food and Circus" that heralded the end and demise of the Roman Empire.

A note about hip injuries in older people that points to about 20% of the health care issue beyond insurance. My father's doctor calmly told him that 90% of hip injuries die within 4 weeks - then left him to go to a doctor's conf. and left him in the hospital without doctor supervision where he promptly caught pneumonia. Even though the hip healed well, he died in a week from the pneumonia.

CHAPTER 25
DAMNED
Letter to the President (1/27/10)

<u>Mass. election and your undivided attention - Imperative to read the important plans of action shown on p. 60.</u>

That was an absolutely fantastic State of the Union talk. You nailed every point and rightfully made them all stick. You called spades, spades, and reset the history in no uncertain terms and language of how we all got here. I would not have wanted to be one of the opposition sitting there with their hands folded staring like they had <u>absolutely no clue of reality</u> of the world they have <u>made for the rest of us to live in totally against our will and at great discomfort</u> and detriment to all of us in the USA as well as the rest of the world. They looked just plain stupid, and frankly, very pathetic!!! What total louts and clouts.

Then, <u>they</u> went to the center of the Old Dominion south and <u>stacked the house with animated cardboard cut outs like Bush used to use on the campaign trail</u> to try to make it look like there are <u>real people</u> out there who are <u>buying the load off the manure truck that they are trying to sell</u>. That speech was <u>as out of touch and pathetic as the one Bobby Jendal</u> unloaded the year before except that they had a "choir" singing the praises, halleluiahs and Amen's so it wouldn't <u>seem as ridiculous</u> or be so obvious that it hadn't a stitch of <u>any reality anywhere in the world</u>!! I wonder if they had <u>to pay</u> the one or two minorities that were prominently planted there. This group is so <u>out of touch with anything real</u> that they don't even know when they look <u>totally ridiculous pretending to be "cool"</u>, omnipotent or inscrutable. Total hypocrites!!

60   Now that I have your attention <u>it is time to look at the book to find the true messages distilled a number of times</u> as much as <u>15 months ago</u>. <u>There are compelling reasons</u> to review these excerpts as they <u>reveal the true reasons for the Tea Bag Parties, the surprise vote in Mass. and the general disgust for the congress</u>. They show the underlying feelings and point to <u>actions that are required</u> to turn <u>this anger around</u> and <u>get back in touch with the America</u> that you <u>set out to save a year ago</u> before you seemed to lose your way!!! <u>These are VERY IMPORTANT!!!!</u>

JOBS, JOBS, THE ECONOMY AND HIGH TECH JOBS

Chapter 2, 10/15/08, Page 5 last para. and page 6.

Chapter 4, 10/26/08, page 9 -12 top & bottom para.

Chapter 6, 11/10/08, page 14, 15 2nd para., 16 bttm par.

And all of 17. All of chapter 7, 11/17/08, pages 18-19.

Chapter 8, 11/18/08, pages 20-21 - unrest & economy.

Chapter 9, 11/23/08, all pages 22-25 – <u>A MUST READ!!!!</u>.

Chapter 10, 11/25/08 all pages 26-27 - <u>A MUST READ!!!!</u>.

Chapter 11, 12/11/08 all pages 28-29 - <u>A MUST READ!!!!</u>.

Chapter 12, 12/25/08 all pages 30-31 - <u>A MUST READ!!!!</u>.

Chapter 13, 1/1/09. page 35, unrest and <u>A MUST READ!!!!</u>.

Chapter 14, 2/9/09, pages 36-37 unrest <u>A MUST READ!!!!</u>.

Chapter 15, 2/28/09, pages 38-39 <u>to do</u> <u>A MUST READ!!!!</u>.

Chapter 16, 3/09/09, pages 40-41 first 2 and last 2 paras.

61

Chapter 17, 6/19/09, pages 42-44 NO and Health Care!!!!

All last chapters 18 – 27, 7/19/09 – 2/16/10 - Health Care, Economy, NO Politics, Unrest, Jobs, All a A MUST READ!!!!.

Our Health Care system was designed by a 6,000 lb Gorilla in a Tiffany's Warehouse!! The opposition talks about "Obama's Experiment". This is pure Bull Shit!! These universal health care systems in the majority of the world are the tried and true systems that have survived the test of time – many, more than 20 years. These are the stable, working and productive health care systems – that time & elections have proven to work for many, many years.

The "experiment" that clearly doesn't work is the health care system in the United States that was designed by the 6,000 lb. Gorilla over the past 60 years and has only gotten worse, not better, and is getting far worse every day! That is the "experiment" that THEY are supporting!!!

PERCEPTION, PERCEPTION, PERCEPTION IS 70% OF WHAT IS NEEDED TO GET THE PUBLIC BACK ON YOUR SIDE AND TO BRING THE INDEPENDENTS BACK. TILL NOW, THE ONLY PERCEPTION THEY HAVE HAD IS THAT YOU ARE CATERING TO THE BIG CORPS, THE BANKS, THE FED, WALL STREET, THE INSURANCE COMPANIES AND THE DRUG COMPANIES!!!! They see that you have forsaken those who voted you in to save us – We The People of these United States. You didn't listen to those who elected you! You didn't pay attention to MAIN STREET who is still hurting very badly!

STOP LISTENING TO THE INSIDERS & GET THE PEOPLE'S PULSE

62   So what happened in Massachusetts? Very simple, it <u>started the day after your tremendous election</u>. <u>You turned those who elected you OFF</u> and went with the old <u>establishment that got all of us into this horrible GD mess</u>. It isn't "Change we can believe in", it's SHAME we can't trust! A TOTAL TRAVESTY - a TOTAL BETRAYAL!! JUST LISTEN!

<u>Health care was the number one priority of those who elected you</u>. You were right to try to get it passed in the first year and deliver on it. What went wrong? You should have spent those months between 11/4/08 and 1/20/09 writing THE health care plan and have it ready to pass up front. You should have <u>told your Party in no uncertain terms</u> that <u>they would vote for it in a block</u> – no ifs ands or butts. (That was not a typo – there were <u>too many Butts</u>!) GW Bush had his health care plan that he ram-rodded through the congress even against his inside opponents. (Oh, golly, was that not a <u>Government Run Health Care plan</u>? Was that not a plan that has run flawlessly since it's inception? <u>How many complaints</u> have we had from the opposition on that <u>Government Run Health Care Plan</u>?)

The media pundits say much about the Mass election. Bottom line? <u>What people were mad about</u> was not that you were trying to pass a health care reform bill, it was about how it was <u>allowed to be screwed up</u> by the corps. the opposition and in particular by totally weird and <u>unscrupulous rascal members of your own Party</u>!!!! They should have been <u>CHEWED A NEW EXIT HOLE</u> from day 1!! YOU SHOULD HAVE BEEN ON TOP OF IT AND NOT LET IT WANDER OR GET OUT OF HAND FROM DAY ONE. <u>IT WAS YOURS TO WIN</u> AND TO ALL OF OURS TO NOT LOSE! WE LOST, BOY DID WE LOSE -AND LOST WITH HURLED CHUNKS!!

You had the votes and initiative and just seemed to look the other way!!! You let the opposition write part of the bill – a bill it was assured that they would not vote for or support. You let the Corps, Drug and Insurance co.'s write part of the bill – a bill that they clearly would not support. You let the Dems who claimed they were saving their butts at home but were actually protecting what they believed to be their clients – the Drug, Insurance and Financial Companies – to demand ridiculous additions. By the time the, what should have been a 10 Page Medicare E bill, become a 2500 page total monstrosity and abortion, everyone at home was so angry at you and the congress that they were either not listening anymore or didn't care any more. They knew that even if it passed, it was no longer for them and worse it would not do any of the things they needed – at least not until 2014 when the opposition would surely kill it. What is more, it had pure crap in it that never belongs in any bill. We needed it last year if not sooner!! They, therefore, voted for a total referendum in Mass. and threw out the BABY WITH THE BATH!!!! Many of your former supporters are actually very happy that it is dead – Finito.

They say a Zebra is a Horse designed by a committee!! However, a Zebra is a useful and very beautiful animal. This Horse/Toad/Snake with a Giraffe head between the legs catastrophe is neither useful nor beautiful and IS NOT THE CHANGE THAT WE WERE TOLD OR SOLD AS ONE WE CAN BELIEVE IN!! WE WERE SIMPLY CHEATED, SEEING THE WORST ABOMINATION OF GOVERNMENT IMAGINABLE!! This was just more of the same that we suffered through under GW Bush. No Change and nothing for Main Street!!!

64   That having been said, it is <u>still far worse to vote for anyone</u> in the <u>ReCorpiCon Group for whatever reason</u>, whether for spite, anger, disgust or simple apathy. The <u>consequences</u> will be <u>not just a repeat of the horrible past 8 year regime</u> but <u>instead become FAR worse because they would have become emboldened by making a come back from a resounding defeat in 2008</u>. See the CHECK LIST, page "v", to <u>re-calibrate on this</u>, and <u>remember who crashed all of our lives, savings, homes, jobs, retirements, national surpluses, markets and caused two costly, unnecessary wars and a world depression of an un-precedented magnitude – all at great benefit to themselves with a price of a TOTAL DETRIMENT to us all.!!!</u>

Just one area has already raised its ugly, catastrophic & distasteful head. The two conservative judges appointed by GW Bush, "<u>who claimed to be moderate</u>" <u>constitution defending judges</u>, not only made a <u>construct entity</u> such as a Corporation into "A Person", but <u>reached far out beyond the case before them</u> and <u>LEGISLATED FROM THE BENCH</u> THAT THESE <u>ARTIFICIAL CONSTRUCTS</u> CAN EXPEND HORRENDOUSLY HUGE SUMS OF CORPORATE MONIES TO CAMPAIGN FOR – OR AGAINST – ANYONE OR ANYTHING THEY CHOOSE RIGHT UP TO AND INCLUDING THE DAY OF THE ELECTION. IF YOU HAD THE FEELING AFTER THAT PAST 8 YEAR DISSASTROUS REGIME THAT WE WERE HEADING FOR <u>FASCISM</u>, <u>YOUR FEELINGS ARE NOW CONFIRED</u>!! WITH THIS DASTARDLY, TOTALLY INSANE DICISION WE HAVE FULLY <u>BECOME A FASCIST GOVERNMENT RULED BY A CABAL OF THE RICHEST MOST INFLUENCIAL PEOPLE IN THE WORLD PURELY FOR THEIR OWN GREED AND SELFISH ENDS. THE GOVERNMENT FOR THE PEOPLE IS NOW A TOTAL FICTION</u>!!!

Why is it that the opposition feels compelled to continually propagandize to their "base" by repeating mistruths, innuendos, slanderous statements about their opposition as if to marginalize and diminish their motives, goals or effectiveness? Are they so _totally insecure about their own capabilities_ that they must "RUN DOWN" their opponents to try to _make themselves look more important or effective_? In truth, it does neither of these things. It just _makes them look sad and pathetic_ and just absurd-ably ineffective. How can anyone "_LEAD_" from the "bully" attitude, of "NO, you are just not going to do that" even if the result will ultimately _be bad for not only us but them as well_? That is not leadership - it is not even governance – good, bad or indifferent!!!! It is just plain stupid!! Why not tell about plans, goals? Oh yes, I forgot!!

I have seen the literature they send out to base. _It's down right scary_. The _most ridiculous_ was an "official" looking FAKE CENSUS QUESTIONAIRE that at least was slanderous and at best totally misleading – using lies as basis for the questions that were presented. When you ask a question like "Do you believe that the Obama Democrats' health care "reform" is more about expanding _socialist power_ than it is about health care?" you are, by implication, _directing_ the emotional response of the reader to focus on "key" reactive trick words like "socialist" and "power" that have predictable responses – whether they are true, relevant or not. The result leaves the _reader_ with a _negative impression_ of the "health care" bill whether they responded or not. When will people wise up to these "obvious" and deliberate tricks to try to make the _Do Nothing,_ ReCorpiCon Group _seem at all relevant_!!!

CHAPTER 26

DAMNED — Letter to the President (2/4/10)

America's best kept secret -- HELL Care not Health Care

We are not only increasingly being refused health care by these so called Health Insurance Companies – that place themselves between the Doctor and the Patient by refusing payment or cancelling the policy but we are now experiencing a new threat from the doctors themselves. More and more doctors are setting up their own "patient" rules and having their patients sign "contracts" that say something like: "If you miss <u>ONE</u> appointment or cancel an appointment within 24 hours of the appointment, you are <u>removed from the practice</u> – forever! That's it, finito, sayonara!! Now, experience that just once with a favorite doctor with whom you have had a decade of a relationship and it throws you for a loop!!

However, far worse, it can <u>and often does</u> lead to serious consequences like not being treated for serious, death risking illnesses at the most crucial time. Add injury to insult, <u>try getting another doctor</u> to see or treat you after that, as there are records that the former doctor keeps and may pass on to any new doctor who will and does look at them with a great deal of fear and trepidation. That is no way to start off on a good footing with a new primary care physician!! I personally know of cases where simple ailments to treat such as bladder infections or intestinal infections went untreated because of that and led to extremely serious consequences such as kidney failure, heart failure, Atrial Fibrillation and stroke.

<u>I should not have to tell you</u>, that a <u>universal health care system would TOTALLY FIX and ELIMINATE THAT KIND OF ARBITRARY TREATMENT OF PATIENTS.</u> KEEP IN MIND THIS KIND OF HELL—CARE HAPPENS WHETHER YOU HAVE INSURANCE OR NOT OR ARE ON MEDICARE OR NOT! THE DOCTORS HAVE BECOME CORP.S AND ENTITIES UNTO AND TOTALLY FOR THEMSELVES!!!   PATIENTS BE DAMNED!!!! The long and the short of it is that despite how much you pay for coverage and despite how much coverage you may have, you <u>can still be totally without health care under the present care system</u> designed by the 6,000 lb. gorilla.

Ironically, our early health care system and in rural areas of the US made sense. The doctor <u>went to the patient at his place of residence and illness</u>. Why did this make sense? The doctor was <u>well</u> and able to travel whereas the patient was sick and likely not able to travel. Now, we as patients, are forced to go to the doctor's office and are <u>severely penalized</u> if we can't make it, or must cancel the appointment at the last minute. Have doctors forgotten why they are doctors? <u>It was to TREAT patients, not BEAT patients - UP</u>. We are to the point where <u>GOLF</u> is far more important than a <u>GALL</u> bladder day at work.

They are going more for the bottom line – all for the Corp. at the total expense of those who are the basis of their profession – <u>the patient who funds their Corporation</u>. It has been no different than Enron, World Com, Wall Street, Phone companies, Drug companies, Insurance co.'s the Banks. It is all for them even if they have to extract it from their "clients" any way they can. <u>We are the DUPED!</u>

68 TAXES, TAXES, TAXES, WHO TRULY RAISED YOUR TAXES?
The CONSTANT NAY SAYERS are perpetually talking about Democrats and Obama going to raise all of our taxes. <u>Tax and Spend, Tax and Spend is their constant mantra</u>. Let's put this in <u>complete perspective</u>!! How many of you had your salary lowered 25 - 30% in the past ReCorpiCon Decade? <u>That IS A PERMANENT TAX INCREASE on the incomes of the middle class for the rest of their lives</u>!! If you work 20 more years, at say $100,000 a year, that amounts to nearly ½ million dollars <u>you have lost to TAXES THAT THE OPPOSITION PLACED UPON YOUR SALARY</u>! Do you know the worst part of that? <u>Not one dime</u> of that helped pay for your government to supply your needs of the Nation or community. <u>Not one dime paid for police,</u> or army or helped this government help you get through this horrendous financial mess that they, the opposition, directly caused. Talk about the <u>Great ReCorpiCon Depression of the 30's</u>, this is the <u>great, record Repression (ReCorpiCon) that broke all of our BACKS for all time</u>!!

Is not a <u>total decimation of your retirements</u>, savings and stocks and bonds a <u>100% TAX</u> on not only your future status, but <u>a huge tax on your entire lifetime of earnings</u>?!

Talk about your retro-active taxes!! This tax is retroactive <u>on your entire lifetime of earnings - from day one till death do us in!! This was a tax brought to bear upon you by your "friends" – you guessed it - the ReCorpiCons</u>!!!!

Is not health care costs doubling every three years a 21% tax on your earnings or those of the company that pays your salary? This is the <u>Present Tax</u> the <u>ReCorpiCons want to perpetuate on your lives and income for all time</u>!! Ever!

Is not having the value of your house and property decrease by 25-35% a retroactive tax on your earnings for all time – all of your life? <u>If you lose your house</u>, it is a 100% tax on all the money that you spent on the house in paying on the principle and interest. That is a <u>huge and un-recoverable TAX ON YOUR LIVES!!!</u> Mark my word, <u>these are no less taxes on our lives and incomes</u> than something we all know and understand like taxes on cigarettes, liquor, property or income. <u>THEY have taxed your earnings, your savings, your livelihoods for all time, your retirements for all time and your lives for all time</u>. Can't but feel that this was all well planned & deliberate!!

Talk about your totally, selective "class based" taxes. These were all on the middle class – Oh, forget about the lower classes – they wrote them off as irrelevant years ago as being totally useless and not worth worrying about. Do you remember, "You're doing a Heck of a Job Brownie". After 4½ years, you may now believe that what was meant was – you are doing a heck of a job doing absolutely nothing for these poor people in New Orleans.

These taxes didn't seem to touch many of the upper classes as their salaries all went up perhaps more than 30% during this past <u>ReCorpiCon Decade</u> along with their home values coupled with a lack <u>of foreclosures</u> in that "class". Besides, they gave themselves a huge tax cut from the federal government during that decade. Keep in mind, they started two wars, one of which was totally unnecessary and <u>did not pay for them</u>. <u>That's a tax on our children, grand children and great grand children</u>. Making these deficits Obama's is a <u>Going to Hell Lie</u>! One must <u>look no further than their past Tax Happy Decade</u>!!

70 These tax increases passed onto us by the last Repub Admin. ARE PERMANENT!! No matter what is done to try to mitigate them, they ARE PERMANENT, RETROACTIVELY FOREVER. They can't be repealed or paid back! THAT MONEY IS JUST GONE – FOREVER. So, you ReCorpiCons, don't cry tax increases, job losses or huge deficits without first pointing to yourselves and saying these ReCorpiCon tax increases, these ReCorpiCon job losses and huge deficits - all ReCorpiCon. If one looks at ALL history it has been the ReCorpiCons that were responsible for these throughout history. You TEA BAGGERS MUST TAKE HEED!!!!!

We've been duped and taxed to DEATH by the meanest, most self serving Louts and Clouts on the Planet and yet still refuse to believe for mysterious reasons that they've done this to us. Tea Baggers, think about your lives. What years were the best of times for you and your families and under which were the absolute worst? Oh, you guessed it -- under the ReCorpiCon years. Remember Reagan's trickle down economics? That was a trickle down to you at a time when the fat cats were getting richer, fat and happy. Tea Baggers, you must take NOTE!!

The worst thing and the most appalling thing is that people here don't seem to pay any attention to any of this! In particular, some of those most at risk of losing everything, and I mean everything, their money, life and freedoms – are the ones who don't even pay attention to the things that are happening all around them that happen every day and will eventually bring them down. You must shout this from the roof tops and get them angry I mean really, really, really angry!!!! We should be Rioting in streets!!! We should be burning them in effigy!!

CHAPTER 27

DAMNED   Letter to the President (2/16/10)

I'M MAD AS HELL AND GETTING MADDER BY THE MINUTE!

Had you been paying attention from the start, you would have spent those months between 11/04/08 and 1/20/09 starting important programs for the people of the United States rather than wasting important lead time "picking" a useless cabinet of "SAME OL, SAME OL, BUSINESS AS USUAL" insiders that have done little to help you help the PEOPLE OF THESE UNITED STATES – THE ONES WHO ELECTED YOU AS WELL AS THE MAJORITY IN THE HOUSE AND SENATE

You needed to have weekly press conferences during that period talking about the things you were going to do to help the plight of MAIN STREET and to start high tech. companies and stimulate job growth. You needed to have weakly broadcast meetings in all the "severely effected" parts of the country like the Rust Belt with a two pronged message!! One, to thank them for their past support to get you elected and continued support to get the important things passed in Congress for them and the USA: Two, to talk about specific programs and bills and actions that you definitely have planned and that are already in the works for their benefit.

You needed to talk long and often about the problems we inherited and exactly what you intended to do about each and every one of them!!! You needed to connect the implications like the need for health care reform to fix a huge drag on the economy. You needed to forget about Bi-Partisanship from the start as it was doomed, not by your genuine efforts but by the plan of the Opposition!

72   This attempt at reconciliation – though perhaps well meant – <u>was seen by those who elected you as caving in to the bas----s that got us all into this mess</u>. It was <u>as though you were cavorting with the enemy</u> – even worse like <u>forgiving them and their incredible insanities that ruined all of our lives</u>. This actually gave <u>rise to the Tea Baggers</u> and was largely responsible for what made them so mad. You see, the Tea Baggers were really YOUR PEOPLE, THE PEOPLE WHO GOT YOU ELECTED - GONE BAD! <u>They are not mad at your attempting to do too much</u>, as many of the Media Pundits claim, <u>but for NOT DOING NEAR ENOUGH TO GET WHAT WE WANTED DONE FOR US</u>!!!

You must realize <u>half</u> of your success at being elected was the incredible <u>hatred</u> for those who caused the <u>black hole</u> of the previous 8 years. The other half was to believe in someone who was committed to changing all of that – FOREVER. As much as it was to do, <u>they needed to see you working on solving THEIR problems from DAY ONE -24/7</u> – IT MEANS <u>FROM 11/04/08</u>!!! You should have <u>declared war on poverty, foreclosures, bankruptcies, job losses on 11/04/08</u> and <u>taken highly visible positive actions do solve them</u>!!!!!!   That means, you should have <u>talked often</u> about what you intended to do about <u>THEIR incredible TAXES</u> - <u>incredible Debt</u> – <u>incredible losses of incomes</u> – <u>incredible losses of retirements, savings stocks and bonds</u> that they had laid on the entire nation in those eight years. Yes, <u>they are now incredibly angry</u>, but their <u>anger was about the opposition</u> and the <u>incredibly hard times</u> that <u>they were left in at the end of those 8 years</u>, but now your <u>apparent inactivity and lack of positive, masterful, bold</u>, WAR TIME steps to fix it have <u>transferred</u>

that anger to you & the congress that was just stupid, 73 I mean the Democrats who were just plain arrogant and incredibly stupid. Everything, if planned from 11/04/08 could have been passed easily in your first year in office.

You should be at each and every Tea Bagger Rally and meeting and talk to them about how you are with them in their pain. These were and could still be your people. You need to keep them working for you instead of working against you. Unfortunately, you may have wasted too much time with your "Goldman Sachs" crowd to have any credibility at all with them. Perhaps a cleaning of "that house" is in order and put some bright, ordinary, very effective, caring people in their places.

You know, there are now several more books planned for next year. At the present time the new titles might be (Finally Being), then (Hoping to be) and unfortunately last (Failing to be) President. God help us all if it comes to that final sequence, It doesn't have to be that way. It could be a much different sequence: (Better at being) and (Finally being) President. However, that would require wholesale changes and a renewed image of decisive, forceful, bold stroke actions to take command and ram rod through what is right for the American People, rather than the American Corps and Banks. CAN the financial types, and DECLARE WAR AND TAKE POSITIVE ACTIONS BY WARTIME EXECUTIVE ORDERS TO FIX THE HEALTH CARE SYSTEM, THE ECONOMY FOR THOSE STRUGGLING AND FOR CREATING JOBS. The only people who will blame you, then, are the small hard core group of the Opposition –they would blame you no matter what you did. Get with the Tea Baggers and fix their ailments!!!

CHAPTER 28

DAMNED — Letter to the President (2/23/10)

I know you have a grand plan, an "audacity of hope", a <u>core belief</u> that you can somehow work with the worst possible people on earth and through <u>logic, discussion, reason & forbearance of cause</u> will ultimately convince them to come to your side. <u>Nice dream</u>, but it's TOTAL CRAP & BULL SHIT! Yes, I SAID IT'S PURE BULL SHIT!!!! <u>These people have but one goal</u> and that <u>goal is to defeat you and the Democrats once and for all</u> and to then by your disgrace and the total disgrace of congress to <u>retake the control of the government in 2010 and the presidency in 2012!!</u> I <u>know this is their goal</u> because I get <u>their literature and "bogus" opinion questionnaires</u>. They state this over and over again – <u>with glee</u> - in their literature!!!!!

Nice Dream, <u>but it is not our dream</u>, the dream of WE THE PEOPLE – by the way, the same <u>WE THE PEOPLE that got you elected!!</u> This <u>NICE CRAP</u> is turning your base off. This <u>playing to the interests of the Insurance companies and Banks is turning your base off</u>. This NICE CRAP of letting the criminals and crooks get off scot free for the <u>total devastating damage they did to not only us here in the USA</u> during that decade, but to the entire world is <u>turning your base totally and completely off!!</u> <u>We were severely harmed and damaged by that crowd with 25% to 35% in PERMANENT taxes</u> on <u>our incomes, savings, homes, jobs, retirements, children's, grand children's and great grand children's future</u> -PERMANENT, IRREVERSIBLE TAX & WORSE YET <u>DID NOT AND WILL NOT PAY FOR ANYTHING WE NEED- SERVICES, POLICE, ARMY, HEALTH CARE, INFRASTRUCTURE. It is just GONE - GONE FOREVER – ROBBED & NO JUSTICE!!!</u>

CHAPTER 29

DAMNED — Letter to the President (2/28/10)

We know you have tried and tried repeatedly to reach out to the other side – a reaching that so far has done nothing more than RUIN OUR HEALTH BILL – a bill that they have NO INTENTION OF SUPPORTING OR WILL VOTE FOR!!

Well, you had your health care summit at Blair House. It should be at this point ABSOLUTELY CLEAR THAT THEY HAVE NO INTENTIONS THAN TOTAL DESTRUCTION OF ANY EFFORT TO ENACT ANY REFORM ON HEALTH CARE DELIVERY OR INSURANCE. HOPEFULLY THE AMERICAN PEOPLE WILL NOW HAVE THE SAME INFORMATION AND ACT ON IT. "OH, WE SEE A NEED FOR REFORM. LET'S START OVER AND DO IT COMPLETELY OUR WAY - A DRIBBLE AT A TIME". EVEN IF YOU LET THEM WRITE THE WHOLE DEAL IN A MONTH AND GET IT TO THE FLOOR, THEY WOULD NOT LAY OUT ONE VOTE TO PASS IT. THEY CANNOT STAND TO HAVE ANYTHING, EVEN SOMETHING THEY WROTE, MAKE YOU OR THIS ADMINISTRATION LOOK GOOD. THEIR INTENTIONS ARE SO TRANSPARENT THAT YOU CAN SEE THROUGH THEM AT MIDNIGHT ON A TOTALLY MOONLESS, FOGGY NIGHT.

Tom Coborn said it all, bless him!! Yes, he was absolutely right in one important point when he said "One dollar out of every three does not go for health care" YOU are RIGHT, Tom, but you failed to say, and the Democrats failed to correct you; One dollar out of three does not go to health care, IT GOES TO PROFITS, ADVERTISING, CORP LOBBYISTS AND CORP EXECUTIVE SALARIES AND BONUSES. YES, TO THE LOUTS AND CLOUTS WHO'S COMPANIES. EARNED 56% MORE IN PROFITS THIS YEAR – A DEPRESSION

76 YEAR & DROPPED 2.7 MILLION MORE PATIENTS FROM COVERAGE AND ARE SPENDING $1.4 MILLION DOLLARS A DAY ON DEFEATING ANY EFFORT TO PASS A REFORM BILL!!! NOW, THEY HAVE THE BALLS TO RAISE RATES 39% ACROSS THE COUNTRY. TALK ABOUT HUBRIS & ARROGANT TIMING!!

TALK ABOUT THE TOTAL ARROGANCE AND UNBELIEVABLE HUBRIS TO DO ALL THIS RIGHT WHEN A BILL IS TRYING TO BE PASSED!! THAT DOES IT! THE INSURANCE COMPANIES HAVE THUMBED THEIR NOSE AT YOU AND THE CONGRESS AT THE WORST TIME!! IF THE AMERICAN PUBLIC DOES NOT NOW SEE THEM AND THEIR SUPPORTERS IN CONGRESS FOR WHAT THEY TRULY ARE, THEN WE AS A NATION ARE COMPLETELY AT RISK OF LOSING EVERYTHING WE HAVE FOUGHT FOR IN OVER 200 YEARS! WHAT HUBRIS - TOTAL UNMITTIGATED HUBRIS AND ARROGANCE! IF NOTHING ELSE, THAT SHOULD PROVE TO ALL THERE'S A NEED TO PASS THIS REFORM BILL!!!

That is RIGHT! What Tom failed to say was that the 1/3 loss of revenue to actually deliver health care is not from the so called Litigation which amounts to about 2-4% of cost. Even so, that could be put in the bill if it is not already there. No need to scrap and start over!! It is not the loss from fraud or crime in Medicare that amounts to about 1-2% of loss. Even so, this is very important, and needs to be pursued with vigor using the district attorneys and law enforcement. It won't, however, ever pay for health care for the 35 – 45 million people out there who desperately need health care YESTERDAY!! Yes, savings perhaps, but there is no way for that to help anyone who needs the help. Make no mistake about it, these pronouncements are no more than attempts to further confuse the public and further delay or defeat any attempt to pass THIS bill!!!

IT IS OBFUSCATION, stupid, just plain **OBFUSCATION!!**
That is all!! They came with nothing more than feeble attempts to claim, fraudulently, but still claim that WE THE PEOPLE do not want this (or essentially this) health care bill to pass NOW IN THE NEXT TWO TO FOUR WEEKS – NOW!

WE FOUGHT TO GET YOU ELECTED – TO PASS THIS BILL. WE BOUGHT AND PAID FOR YOU AND MANY, MANY MORE TO BE ELECTED TO DO JUST ONE THING – TO PASS THIS BILL. IF WE ARE UPSET, IT IS THAT NOT ENOUGH HAS BEEN DONE TO PASS THIS BILL, RATHER THAN THAT YOU HAVE TAKEN ON TOO MUCH, AS THE RECORPICON MEDIA PUNDITS CLAIM. You need to get this passed and to be effective now. They have already done too much damage to it and it's ultimate effectiveness. They have already given away the store to the Drug and Insurance companies – and for what? For WE THE PEOPLE OF THESE UNITED STATES? HELL NO! But politics is still just that, politics and just a good bill is far better than NON AT ALL!! GET IT DONE AND NOW!!!

Another thought about our present health care system designed by the 6000 lb gorilla at Tiffany's. Even with health coverage, we (mainly men) don't want to go to the doctor or have any tests unless we are about to just plain croak. It's not that we just don't care – it is far more serious than that. We have to work to pay the bills, keep the family going, keep a roof over our family's head. We have responsibility for the lives of many other people. (Of course this applies to women as well.) The results from the tests far too often have serious consequences. They can deny Life Ins coverage, change our job or promotion prospects and prevent many more important things from happening. Something is just plain wrong about this!!!!

CHAPTER 30
<u>DAMNED</u>   Letter to the President (3/08/10)

Do you know that in the end (and even in the beginning) there was only one way to deal with Hitler and that was to beat him mercilessly at his own game and do that with overwhelming force, stealth, cunning while allying with others with strengths and background. Chamberlain tried to capitulate with Hitler and we all know how that turned out. It seems that there are just some people like Al Quida and others we know, who have by <u>design</u> and <u>pledge</u> to a goal or mantra to do everything they can to defeat any and all things that we do. If you push here, they will push there. They are by intellect or belief system BOUND to be opposed to EVERYTHING THAT YOU DO, <u>NO MATTER HOW BADLY IT SERVES THEM OR DAMAGES THEM ULTIMATELY IN THE END</u>. They <u>never negotiate</u>, they only <u>appear to be negotiating</u>. <u>They do not yield</u> even though they may <u>appear to be yielding</u>. History is an excellent teacher to those who have lived through it and studied it.

It is <u>clear to all of us</u> out here including the <u>Tea Baggers</u> that there seems to be <u>one Party</u> that basically <u>has</u> at least some of <u>the interests of WE THE PEOPLE at heart</u>. They sometimes get lost in the details or are distracted by <u>money that should have no place in these decisions</u>, but at least, <u>they are basically working for WE THE PEOPLE</u>.

Our recent <u>past decade</u> has taught most of us a <u>very painful, costly, destructive lesson. That lesson should be "BURNED" into the minds, brains and psyches of every citizen of these United States for at least the next 50 years. When ReCorpiCons work</u> for their <u>own personal</u> or ideological goals or ends, they are clearly not serving WE THE PEOPLE the basis for this government and its ONLY REASON FOR BEING!! When the goal may be primarily to take control of a government that they PROFESS TO HAVE ABSOLUTELY NO NEED FOR AT ALL they show themselves as the total hypocrites that they appear to be. If in fact they believe that a strong central government is bad, or that the central government cannot do anything right, or that any government is only a detriment to all that really matters – totally unfettered, unregulated, unencumbered businesses – then why are they so hell bent on taking total control of this purely useless entity?! It just boggles the mind to try to make sense of that absurd reasoning.

We hear talk about how bad it is for judges to "Legislate from the Bench" and yet that is exactly what their judges do. We hear about how bad Lawyers, Litigation and Law suits are, and yet they rely on their lawyers to do most of the litigation and law suits against all others. We hear how reducing taxes is a cure-all for everything, yet they insist on having Interstate highways and bailouts for disasters. They are the first to complain when food is found to be poisoning people, bridges collapse, toys come into the country with lead paint and airlines are attacked or have accidents. These examples aren't built by hack, hammer, hope nor can they be regulated or maintained by just state or city governments alone. They say our military and it's equipment is the best in the world – bar non. Is that not a huge government run organization? Even the present government run health care and retirement programs run totally flawlessly and effectively. What about the VA hospital system? If they think it is so bad, then why don't they make a fuss to fix it for their precious soldiers whom they claim to totally support? If states rights are so important, why did they implore the US Supreme Court to over-rule in a clearly States Rights Issue – Elections in 2000? Bah Humbug!!

Without much trouble one could go on for 10 or 20 more pages with more examples of apparent paradoxes in the difference between their "WORDS" AND THEIR "ACTIONS" or their "WORDS" AND THEIR "TRUE BELIEFS"! Have they forgotten why the pilgrims came to this land in the first place? It was to escape a rule by the few against the many and to escape from religious persecution. The constitution was based upon a very strong separation of church and state and for very good reasons based upon their past experiences. They guaranteed that everyone could believe or pray any way they wanted, but that it was NOT TO BE MADE official, or by any other method, any part of the government. There can be no religious tests for any office or any other position in government!!!!!

Now, we have just experienced at length the earthquake in Haiti and now Chili. According to a book on Sudden Theory such situations fall under the category of Pleasure turned in an instant to Pure Hell by crossing a line in time. In the case of Haiti, it was not much pleasure before but that is immaterial to the point being made. Suddenly, in a matter of a minute, hundreds of thousands of people are dead or trapped under tons of concrete or stone. Thousands are hurt or harmed for life, if they are so lucky to even survive. What is needed instantly on a massive scale is Food, Water, Distribution and Medical and

Surgical Care on a scale that is just mind boggling. No city or small state government can handle that alone.

Yet, to meet the humanitarian need, it MUST BE handled by an overriding huge organization to meet the need!

Oh yes, did you note that the absolute needs of these thousands of people are Food, Water and Medical attention – especially Surgery? It turns out that these are the minimal, basic needs of everyone on earth but are critical at times like this for everyone - even the poorest people of Haiti. We all responded to this because not only is this a fundamental need that we all recognize – a basic right – not just for those in disaster - but for all those everywhere, in all situations, throughout their entire lives.

This sudden "rush to humanitarianism" shouldn't be just a goal for an emergency but for all time, all times and all peoples. Thus, the message is that the basic needs of all peoples – Food, Water, Shelter and good Health Care for all - should be considered an absolute need for all times and all situations. It should not be just an on again, off again, for foreigners only, short term commitment!! It must be a constant for our psyche and care. It must be done for the basic humanitarian spirit in all of us in the US!

By the way, the usual phrase for those poor unfortunates who have just lost their jobs or houses is: Take COMFORT, you are not alone!! Try telling that to someone lying helpless under a two ton slab of concrete!! Somehow, knowing that a hundred thousand other people are also lying, dying under two ton slabs of concrete is not very helpful and certainly not at all comforting. Humanitarian feelings require action not words. We have yet to see the

82   <u>action here at home</u> and it must be done or all is lost for this great nation. Notice also that <u>money</u> in the case of Haiti or Chili <u>is not the issue</u>. However, it became the issue in New Orleans, did it not? <u>They just couldn't "find" the funds for that recovery!!</u> Yet they did for the Iraq War!! They spent <u>$12 Billion a month</u> as a <u>TAX</u> on <u>our Children, Grand Children and Great Grand Children</u> – taking the budget from a <u>$4 Trillion surplus to a $4 Trillion deficit</u> that <u>they passed on</u> with seeming glee <u>to the rest of us to fix</u>. <u>Don't tell us about huge deficits</u>, <u>They're the MAIN CAUSE!</u>

Why must compassion be turned on and off and just for foreign countries, primarily, and for only short periods of time? I guess they figure that the <u>middle class</u> can only afford to help others for short periods of time, and then only <u>others than us</u> - the WE THE PEOPLE! Short sighted compassion equates to Short Sighted Christian Love – or <u>CHRISTIAN COMPASSION ON A BUDGET</u>! Christian Love on a budget – <u>with Greed as it's overwhelming motivation</u> - and mode of operation – or modus operandi! Operation "virtue"!! We have people dying in the streets - 45,000 a year – <u>123 a day or FIVE EVERY HOUR – from lack of useful, affordable health care and/or insurance reforms</u>!!!

How many are out of work, homeless or without health ins as a result of the previous 8 yr. black hole? Three or four million were put out of work – lost their jobs not just for a month, but many for years – during that black hole alone and a couple of million have subsequently lost their jobs since <u>directly as a result of that period</u> and its long lasting effects. They have put an essentially <u>PERMANENT TAX</u>, a non refundable, non repeal able tax on <u>a huge segment of America</u> as the result of <u>politics and greed from Then</u>.

In the case of Haiti/Chili we could not see it coming and therefore were not able to be prepared for it. On the other hand, <u>we did know the financial crisis was coming</u>. <u>We saw for at least two years</u> that there were definite signs to bankrupt this country for their own direct benefit. I read an article in a Money magazine at least <u>three yrs before 2008 that warned about the almost certain total collapse of our substantial financial foundations</u> due to the <u>unregulated OTC derivatives</u> and the false housing bubble that had <u>been created without financial backing and support</u>. We should have been not only aware, but <u>doing something about it – like exposing it, regulating it, and implementing plans to prevent its happening</u>.

Instead, those who were getting incredibly rich from it had <u>absolutely no conscience and certainly no interest in doing anything to prevent</u> those who were the most vulnerable and absolutely in line to lose the most -to lose from these risky money deals. The DEAL was to keep it going as long as possible and RIP OFF as much of the middle class monies – <u>A HUGE TAX ON ALL THEIR MONIES</u> - as could be taken. As a result, they left not only the US but the <u>entire world in a huge financial mess</u> – a nearly world wide depression!! Now they are <u>using the effects of this depression</u> – that they created with greed and glee – <u>to beat up the Democrats</u> who are doing everything in their power to mitigate the effects of this depression that was neither created by the Democrats nor benefited from it!!! TOTAL HYPOCRISY, JUST TOTAL HYPOCRISY! <u>Y'all be DAMNED if we cannot, YOU CANNOT do everything to stop this scam</u>. Call a spade a spade and make it stick. <u>Shout about these ReCorpricon TAXES and RIP OFF's</u>!

84   Because there are a number of things that can <u>harm people suddenly</u> – like a heart attack, or an automobile accident – the only way to effectively mitigate against them is to have the <u>public prepared with health care for all that is available and affordable for all</u>. You see, as with <u>Sudden Theory</u>, we are all being bombarded in a far too increasing progression with situations that <u>can take us from Heaven to Hell in JUST AN INSTANT</u>. We can have worked hard our entire lives, lived frugally and saved for our futures, and just one accident, one heart attack, one job loss, one foreclosure <u>takes everything away with no possibility of ever getting it back</u>. <u>No one should ever have to live that way or with that constant fear that takes us all to the brink on a daily basis</u>. We have lived with that and in that way for <u>not only the past decade</u>, but for the <u>past 60 years waiting for this situation to be fixed</u>.

Just as money begets more money does their greed beget just more and more greed? Are there no limits to <u>their cynicism, grasp at total power, control and greed</u>? <u>How would Christ view this situation</u>? How can anyone who has been "<u>bought off by the Corporate power and greed</u>" still believe they are <u>following Christ</u>? Remember what Christ did to the money changers in the Temple? Sometime this American Taliban has to meet it's maker and have their total "Rupture" – pun intended. <u>It has got to stop</u> or what we all believed to be an America we all could be proud of, and would gladly fight for defend and die for will no longer exist. Talk about your <u>Sudden Theory we are so close to that brink</u> that what little we may call "Heaven" now could be <u>Hell</u> within years <u>months or days</u>. <u>We need to take back the CONTROL AND THE MESSAGE</u>!!

Those who are on Meet the Press & Face the Nation etc. are continually allowed to lie again and again about their so called statistics that "America is not behind the passing of this health care bill". That is not only a crock, it is a pure fabrication – a total fiction spouted to promote Nazi Germany like Propaganda – with the premise that if you say a lie often enough and consistently enough you will make the general un-informed public believe it. The fact that they do not back qny of these "facts" up with any real surveys underscores the dubious nature of these claims. It is now your role to take them to task on these claims. I see that you have finally started to do just that!!

Do you know, it is so ludicrous the specious "arguments" that these talking heads put up as reasons to not pass this bill. "If you Democrats succeed in passing this bill using "reconciliation" that will invite ridicule and you will be defeated in November". The total absurdity of this is that If that is true, then why wouldn't they gleefully want the Democrats to proceed and just let it happen? Why act concerned that it may happen? (Reconciliation is a technique they often used to pass the huge tax cut for the rich, the Medicare part D for retirees, and many others that went against the public interests.) What happened to their constant Mantra in the past decade of "Just an UP or DOWN vote" - America deserves it. They must really want this bill killed. The corporations and insurance companies must really want this bill killed. Their arguments, then, are all the more justification to get it passed by whatever means and processes available to do it. THAT GROUP AND CORPS MUST BE STOPPED NOW! They give us the REASONS to do it every day and way!!!!!!

86 Y'all be DAMNED SCOURGE: the RIP-CORP-OFF-CONs.

There could be other forms, ReCorpiCon, ReCorpRipCon, RipCorpiCon, ReCorpliCon, RipCorpiCon and so on and so forth. At the least, we have seen throughout these pages many references to <u>the Incredible Strangle Hold</u> that the ReCorpiCons have over our lives. We have experienced in not just the past decade where it was INTENSE, but since the Reagan years, <u>the continual erosion of our Democracy</u> by Corporations and other such interests <u>to form a more perfect FASCIST UNION</u>. The constitution might as well say; We, the Corporations of the United States, in order to form a more perfect FASCIST union, establish Corporate Justice – etc. etc. – do ordain and establish this Corporate Constitution for the United Corporations of America. The last supreme court put the Cap Stone on that one with the ruling about <u>Corporations being People and having total rights to free speech</u> including spending horrendous sums of money to influence election campaigns for or <u>against reformers trying to reform and regulate</u> what else? – <u>Corporations</u>!!!

It's not Rocket Science to know how that will effect the <u>future of this NOW Struggling Democracy</u>. We see in the Congress every day how the Corporate interests already, <u>consistently TRUMP the Public Interests and the will of the People</u>. Look at the present health care bill. The <u>Universal Health Care was a BIG plank of the Democratic Party</u>. We couldn't even get a subset of this – the Public Option – to even be considered by the democratically controlled committee writing the bill. This was at a time when 85% of Democrats and <u>65% of all voters were for it</u>. <u>Daily, the Corp. interests spend millions to kill it</u> almost successfully.

It is absolutely baffling why 80% of those buying into the ReCorpiCon Idiotology are also the ones most ripped off by it and YET have somehow bought off on it being someone else's fault. I heard a yokel the other day defending corporations as being good because we all work for corporations in one way or another. That doesn't mean they have a soul or conscience when it comes to social responsibility. They have but one motive, PROFITS. The BLACK HOLE of the past 10 yrs should have BURNED IT into everyone's brain who/what bankrupted the country (world), reduced their salaries, took their jobs, stole their houses/value and destroyed their retirements & savings!!!

Everyone should have seen a made for TV movie I saw years ago. It was about 2 Chinese brothers - one an excellent Violinist – the other a Karate expert – who were part of a protest like Tiananmen's sq. Their father got them out of the country on a freighter to LA. before they were caught. In the US, the violinist joined a symphony in LA while his brother joined an Asian gang. The gang philosophy was Capitalism at it Best – total Laissez Faire – anything goes!! Yes, it was capitalism at the extreme that it takes when there are absolutely no regulations or regulators. It was very violent and left such an impression about where things could easily go without regulation. It is like what is going on in Juarez with the drug gangs – total Laissez Faire – totally unregulated capitalism. That is where capitalism is headed and is well on the way if what we saw on Wall Street with the OTC Derivatives markets that bankrupted the country is any measure. WE must not allow this to happen. THIS is our only CHANCE to stop it and get the public back on our side & in control!!!!

CHAPTER 31

<u>DAMNED</u> Letter to the President (3/23/10)

<u>GLORY BE and HALLELUIAHS</u>!!!! You don't know it, we both dodged the bullet at about the same time when the health care bill was passed in the House. <u>My wife was so close to death that she could have died</u> had I not been able to get her to the hospital <u>Emergency Room</u> this afternoon. She had <u>severe chest pains and was not able to get a breath</u>. The irony is that she and we and I could <u>still be near death</u> as a result – a <u>slow or quick financial DEATH</u>. <u>Without</u> SINGLE PAYER / UNIVERSAL HEALTH CARE even with Medicare, if this continues, we could face RUIN within a matter of months, forcing me to lose my job, our house, our savings (what little there is) or any hope of a retirement. Forget the retirement - that is already gone which is why I <u>must work at a basic minimum wage job until I die</u>. (After having been a PhD scientist developing some of the most commonly used and exciting product developments of our time.) What a total come down.

<u>Human nature</u> sure comes to the fore when we have this kind of important legislation at risk. The true <u>nature and character</u> of the Louts and Clouts of the ReCorpiCons sure comes out at a time like this!!!! I have never heard such <u>mean spirited Rancor</u>, Rationalization, Hubris, Lying, Posturing, Propaganda, Deception, Obfuscation, not to mention just plain old fashioned Pontification!!! What total Louts and Clouts!!! <u>45,000 are dying</u> without health care every year – 123 a day – <u>FIVE every hour</u>, FIFTEEN X's THE NUMBER KILLED ON 911!!! <u>THE IRAQ WAR WOULD HAVE PAID FOR HEALTH CARE FOR ALL AND NOT KILLED 100,000 people in the bargain</u>!! See Pg 12 btm par. (Trying to Be).

* THIS IS A BIG F------ DEAL. YOU'RE D--- RIGHT IT IS!!

*The fact that it was able to be signed at all, a victory for WE THE PEOPLE OF THESE UNITED STATES who ELECTED YOU FOR JUST THIS PURPOSE to pass A BILL TO FINALLY HELP THE – WE THE PEOPLE – INSTEAD OF THE Corporations - is a testament to how hard the ReCorpiCons tried to defeat it – and in so doing were responsible for it's very passage!!!

This really sheds a great deal of light on the 'sincerity' of their ploy, that all that was needed was to scrap this one and start completely over and do it right – THEIR WAY!!! Fat chance after they had at least those LAST 8 Years to do it and they didn't even propose it!!! Oh Yes, lest we forget they passed the Medicare part D – a Government Run Health program - during those years using the same Reconciliation process. Their 15 minute vote at midnight ran over an hour to twist all their arms to get it passed. They HID the cost and didn't provide means to pay for it!!

90   * Ah, yes it is finally done now with the changes!!!!

That having been said and done, you might consider the following surprising train of thought. The alligator tears the opposition Is crying, may just be ones they are crying all the way to the BANK!! With all this bill does for the WE THE PEOPLE it may just do far more for the Drug and Insurance co.s!!! They seem to have gotten all of the financial gains and since their stocks all went up the day the bill was signed – it would seem to confirm they may be the real winners. That would be a WIN WIN FOR THEM AND A PART WIN FOR US. With these very partisan politics, this may be the best that could be expected at this point in time!!!!

Back to this, there are some disturbing possibilities that may have occurred. With the premise that if you want something to succeed, mount a TOTAL opposition against it so those pushing it will be more determined to finish it!!

Looking back at the series of events and oppositions before it, one might conclude that this may have been part of a grand plan. Consider the possible advantages to their side. By being so openly and consistently united against it, they may have ensured its passage with every ReCorpiCon goody and benefit for their corp. interests by making it appear that compromise may get it passed in a bipartisan way. They are having their cake and eating it too! Deep down, secretly, they may be loving it AND also exploiting it for their dastardly ends in November!!

Then the double wammy - the double win, is that by that very same united and consistent push against it, it allows them to make a huge issue about how it was passed and how America doesn't want it and how bad it is for America etc. until the elections in November. But, this kind of Machiavellian tactic can be a two edged sword – that cuts both ways. They run the certain risk that it can all back fire and America gets very tired very fast of their machinations and obvious tactics to smear with half truths, non truths and out and out lies, the issues and end up so very much on the wrong side of Public Opinion!!

A DEFINITION: Re-Corp-I-Con.   Re (again or still) Corp (Corporatists, or for corporations) I (or Y, and) Con (the Con of Pro & Con or more the Con as in Con Game)

"Anyone who uses the premise that what is best for the Corporations is Best for the Nation". Corollary: "Whatever is good for America must be by definition - very good for the Corporations".

Just a thought, Old age is a time in life we cannot ever look back on with fondness, nostalgia or good feelings!!!

92   WHAT IS A CORPORATION? IS IT HUMAN? A PERSON?

A Conscience, A Soul, A Regard for others, Love, Compassion, Being Born (a condition of birth) and an Absolute Death - as one dies by just plain natural causes of having lived a Biological Life Span, ascension to Heaven or Hell, <u>are absolutely associated with PEOPLE</u>, but <u>have absolutely nothing to do</u> - by any stretch of the imagination - <u>with Corporations</u>! Corporations have none of these things and will never have any of these necessary attributes to be considered a person!!! You would therefore think that the Truly Conservative Group would BE <u>ABSOLUTELY OUTRAGED</u> THAT <u>ANYONE WOULD OR COULD EVEN SUGGEST</u> THAT A CORP. <u>COULD BE CONSIDERED A PERSON</u> FOR EVEN THESE FEW OBVIOUS REASONS - WHILE IGNORING THE MANY HUNDREDS OF RELEVANT OTHERS THAT WOULD PRECLUDE IT HAPPENING!!!

<u>People</u> have the right to vote at a certain age, Corps. do not have that right – <u>which would make it impossible and therefore clear that they are not and cannot be People</u>. And yet this very same Crowd seems to <u>JUMP WITH GLEE</u> when the "impartial" and "constitution defending" judges the ReCorpiCons added to the Supreme Court decided to <u>LEGISLATE FROM THE BENCH</u> AND <u>REVERSE A 100 YEAR OLD PRECEDENT</u> AND MAKE <u>CORPORATIONS – PERSONS</u> SO THAT THEY CAN SPEND THE <u>HORRENDOUS SUMS</u> OF DISCRETIONARY <u>MONIES</u> AVAILABLE TO THEM TO <u>RUN ADDS AGAINST ANYONE</u> WHO MAY <u>WANT TO REGULATE THEM OR TO LEGISLATE AGAINST THEM. WELL, ISN'T THAT JUST SPECIAL!!! ISN'T THAT CONVENIENT?!! HYPOCRITES!!!!! It's hard enough for mere humans to raise $100,000 from other people to run for office. Weigh that against Millions!</u>

That doesn't just tip the playing field, it turns it completely on it's end!!! While a candidate must spend most of their time trying to raise, @ $100 a person, the needed funds to just get on the air and campaign - corporations can just take millions out of profits or other discretionary funds and blast away in the media till way past when the cows come home!!! This is perhaps the most insidious non democratic "FIX" TO ENSURE THAT THE COUNTRY IS RUN ENTIRELY BY AND FOR CORPORATIONS AND HANG THE 'so called" "WE THE PEOPLE" THE CONSTITUTION WAS WRITTEN TO PROTECT AND WHICH WAS FOR THEIR DIRECT BENEFIT!!!

THIS, THEN, IN ESSENCE IS HOW Y'ALL BE DAMNED EMPOWERED BY ONE SIMPLE ACT PERFORMED BY NO MORE THAN 5 PEOPLE (out of the 350 million) WHO WERE LEGISLATING FROM THE BENCH!!! IN THIS SIMPLE ACT, THEY MADE LAW THAT HAD FAR REACHING IMPLICATIONS TO CHANGE A BASIC DEMOCRACY INTO A FASCIST STATE BY BYPASSING THE BENEFIT OF ANY PEOPLE VOTING FOR REPRESENTATIVES OR SENATORS!!!! JUST THAT FACT ALONE SHOULD MAKE IT ABSOLUTELY UNCONSTITUIONAL!!!! BUT GUESS WHAT? IT WOULD BE THAT SAME "MODERATE", "UNBIASED", "CONSTITUTIONALLY MINDED" FIVE PEOPLE WHO WOULD DECIDE THE CONSTITUTIONALITY OF EVEN THAT DECISION. THE BOTTOM LINE? THE FIX IS VERY CLEARLY IN!!! EVEN THE HIGHEST COURT IN THE LAND IS INCAPABLE OF RIGHTING THIS ACT - THAT REMINDS MANY OF US OF SOME OF THE EVENTS IN PRE 1940 GERMANY. WHY IS IT THAT IN PAKISTAN, IRAN, BURMA, ETC. IT IS THE CHIEF JUSTICES THAT ARE REPLACED BEFORE REVOLUTION?

94   Well, <u>it seems to go totally against their standards, their moral principles</u> but apparently if it fits their ENDS they seem to <u>overlook the principle of the thing for their own benefit</u> – <u>something they almost never do for anyone else</u>. Could this really be part of the American Taliban? They seem to <u>eschew principle for convenient advantages</u> in order to seek total dominance. What total hypocrites!! It just saddens me! <u>It saddens all of America</u>!

Of the <u>top ten</u> reasons a <u>corporation cannot possibly be a person</u> we consider the following two: <u>profit motive</u> and a <u>compassion for others</u>. These <u>two attributes</u> will <u>never mix</u> – they're mutually exclusive sets – ie. <u>they are always exclusively opposed to each other and cannot exist in the same entity!</u> <u>One belongs</u> exclusively <u>to Corporations</u> while <u>the other</u> exclusively <u>to people</u>. This is the same reason that it is <u>**NEVER WISE to privatize caring/nurturing functions**</u> (humanitarian recovery agencies, education, public protection, disaster, libraries) <u>of any government</u>!! It was largely the profit motive that kept privatized agencies from being very effective at humanitarian efforts in New Orleans. When it came <u>time for immediate action</u>, <u>the profit motive kicked in</u> and effective action and aid were slowed down <u>to a trickle or denied</u> as it **<u>COST TOO MUCH and REDUCED THE BOTTOM LINE</u>**. These privatized functions could never replace government run agencies charged with these services because <u>their criteria for measuring SUCCESS are totally at opposite ends of the scale</u>. One measures <u>the profit</u>, the other measures <u>the actual success</u> of the beneficial effort. For this reason, it is <u>abundantly clear that a person cannot be the same entity as a human construct - a corporation</u>.

This raises a very interesting Corollary: A group that is basically for the benefit of Corporations and is for the ultimate <u>survival of Corporations</u> – <u>by definition</u> – <u>cannot be for people</u>, or <u>WE THE PEOPLE OF THE UNITED STATES</u>. On the other hand, <u>any group that is striving to benefit</u> the <u>WE THE PEOPLE OF THESE UNITED STATES</u> often finds that it runs <u>contrary to the interests of large Corporations</u>. If my representatives or I had a choice in the matter, <u>it would always be on the side of WE THE PEOPLE OF THESE UNITED STATES BECAUSE THAT WOULD PLACE IT 90% on the RIGHT SIDE OF THE CONSTITUTION OF THESE UNITED STATES</u>.

That is why the ReCorpiCons seem <u>always</u> for the bottom line, <u>the most BUCK for the BANG</u>, Less Government, LOWER TAXES! THERE SEEMS TO BE LITTLE COMPASSION for anything or anyone else – <u>it is just not in the CORPORATE interests</u>. The HUGE irony is that if it were just up to the corporatists, there would be perhaps only 20% of the population behind them. As a result they have had to co-opt into other factions and interests to try to attract a broader segment of the population. Ironically the <u>basic tenants</u> of the group, by definition, <u>run counter to the interests of the larger co-opted segments in that group</u>.

Now to the Tea Baggers. They were brought into the fray <u>because they are very, very upset about the things</u> the ReCorpiCons <u>did to them in the past decade. Because of these false co-opt associations</u>, they have been <u>led to believe</u> it was <u>done to them</u> by the people <u>who are trying to fix it for them</u> - now. <u>They are doing themselves in by following these false prophets to their ultimate demise!</u>
*(Pictures from the Public Domain are by Win McNamee and Alex Wong respectively both of Getty Images.)

96   ADDENDUM BASED ON RECENT EVENTS TILL 4/15/10

Oh, there are those times <u>when it seems that you are so right</u> so much <u>before anyone else gets the picture</u>, <u>that you just cannot stand it</u>!!! Then after time, you begin to doubt the validity that was stated 1½ yrs. ago. But when you are vindicated, the feeling is just overwhelming! Take a look at some of the items that were written as early as (10/13/08). As stated in the preface – these were written at the time indicated at the beginning of each chapter. See Chapters 1-5, (10/26/08, 11/4/08) where the <u>reality</u> of being a 'Maverick' is clearly <u>spelled out</u>! I see CNN was so <u>**SHOCKED**</u> at the revelations that they ran numerous clips taken during the campaign showing the "Maverick" claims over and over again! I DON'T THINK I HAVE TO SAY THAT THERE SEEMS TO BE <u>A TOTAL DISCONNECT HERE</u>!

<u>A real question is raised here</u>! Was it a "<u>Maverick</u>" <u>then</u> or would we be subjected to what was suggested in the above pages? Could the talk of <u>being a 'Maverick</u>' been ONLY a MESSAGE of CONVENIENCE? <u>This is truly troubling</u> as what seems to be claimed now is that the "Maverick" never happened! What <u>CAN</u> we believe? What <u>can be believed</u> in this present ENVIRONMENT of campaigns? You be the judge of that!! But, before you do, just stop and think for a moment what a total travesty it could be now if the election had gone another way!! Is this just <u>one more manifestation</u> of the <u>real ReCorpiCon agenda, strategy and tactics</u> <u>to win for all time</u> and for <u>total control</u> of <u>our lives and government</u>? <u>Y'ALL BE DAMNED</u>!!!

I believe the phrase of choice is '<u>just REDUCE the TAXES on the RICH</u>' and <u>all problems will be SOLVED post haste</u>!

Job, employment, giant oil spill, good health, <u>DEFICITS</u>, 97 business prosperity, universal health insurance, fixing Katrina, Haitian earthquake. Chilean earthquake, Global Warming, Energy Supply, Health Insurance for those 35 million without health insurance, 45,000 who die (<u>5 every hour</u>) from <u>CORPORATE GREED</u> by being denied health insurance by <u>the private</u>, <u>for profit health insurance companies</u>, <u>2 wars</u> - <u>all this can be fixed by the simple MANTRA of: just REDUCE TAXES FOR THE RICH</u>!! YEH, RIGHT!

WELL, I HAVE NEWS FOR YOU, IT DOESN'T TAKE <u>A ROCKET SCIENTIST</u> TO UNDERSTAND THIS SIMPLE EQUATION! <u>INPUT MINUS OUTPUT EQUALS THE BALANCE</u>! EVEN IF IT'S CLEAR, LET ME <u>SAY IT</u> AGAIN! <u>INPUT(TAXES) – OUTPUT(SERVICES) = BALANCE (SURPLUS OR DEFICIT)</u>. WITH +60% OF THE EXPENSES FIXED, WHEN YOU REDUCE TAXES FOR CORPS. AND THE RICH (CUTTING INPUT) IT CAUSES THE BALANCE (A PRE 2000 SURPLUS) TO DECREASE UNTIL YOU HAVE A HUGE 2008 DEFICIT! THEN, WHEN YOU <u>INCREASE THE VARIABLE EXPENSES MANY FOLD</u> WITH USELESS WARS AND A PURPOSEFUL BANKRUPTING OF THE MIDDLE CLASS THE DEFICIT GOES SKYROCKETING TO MORE THAN 5 TRILLION DOLLARS THAT SADDLED THE OBAMA ADMINISTRATION! <u>IS THAT HARD TO UNDERSTAND EVEN BY THE LOWEST LEVEL?</u>

THIS HUGE <u>DEFICIT WOULD BE FIXED OR GREATLY REDUCED QUICKLY</u> IF THE CORPS. STILL PAID THE 45-55% OF ALL TAXES COLLECTED THAT THEY USED TO PAY INSTEAD OF THE SMALL AMOUNT THEY PAY NOW OR IF <u>THE RICH PAID WHAT THEY PAID UNDER RONALD REAGAN!! THE REAL REASON WE HAVE SUCH A LARGE DEFICIT</u> IS; 1. THE HUGE ReCORPiCon <u>SPENDING</u> IN THE 8 YEAR PREVIOUS BLACK HOLE, AND THE <u>NOW BANKRUPT MIDDLE CLASS</u> IS FORCED

98   TO PAY THE BULK OF ALL TAXES AND THEY DON'T HAVE MONEY ANYMORE NOR ARE THEY MAKING WHAT THEY USED TO MAKE 10 YEARS AGO!! EVEN NOW THEY ARE HAVING TO WORK HARDER AND LONGER AT TWO JOBS JUST TO KEEP FROM GOING UNDER! TAXES SIMPLY HAVE TO BE PAID TO BRING DOWN THE DEFICIT!! ReCorpiCons HAVE GOTTEN OFF SCOTT FREE AND NOW IT'S TIME TO PAY THE PIPER!! IT JUST DOESN'T TAKE A ROCKET SCIENTIST TO GET THIS AND FIGURE THAT OUT! IT IS JUST THAT SIMPLE!!!

Part of the ReCorpiCon agenda was to take away all of the discretionary and surplus money of the middle class that had gotten all too powerful during the Clinton years. They were investing the surplus and making huge sums of money in a rising market - money they used to influence elections. They were starting tons of new companies that were exceedingly successful (part of the Dot.Com boom) and making huge amounts of money that was put to work on elections. This was exceedingly dangerous to the ReCorpiCon agenda to take over the government. They were so successful at that plan that they nearly bankrupted the entire world in the process. Second rule: when money disappears one place, it doesn't just go away, it shows up somewhere else. I will give you only one guess where that is! It surely is not in the hands of the Tea Baggers or the duped conservative religious groups that seemingly, mysteriously support the ReCorpiCon agenda. Look at the people who are leading those groups around by the NOSE – they aren't the poor people that tend to populate those groups. They're being led by these "folksy", You Betcha speaking icons in sheep's clothing into the slaughter bins of the ReCorpiCons. It is not only pathetic, its truly CRIMINAL! First they dummy down that population and then they use that stupidity to control them to do their bidding and dirty work. They are the ones who are truly HAD, as all the rest of us out here already know what the ReCorpiCons are up to and know the consequences and know to try to buck it in any way that we can and try to put a total stop to it. If we don't – and we only have this one chance to do it under the man we elected to lead us into the battle to do that – then America as a major, strong, vibrant power is truly doomed and cannot exist as a viable beacon of Democracy in the World. We will become the Fascist government that we all should fear far more than the remote terrorists or those outside the US who would try to harm us. We have become the enemy of ourselves and we don't seem to know it. The true enemy is within. Or as said, "we have met the enemy and they are ourselves".

Speaking about this, the Tea Baggers remind us of some of the things going on in the "Forties". There were gangs of people who intimidated well meaning people of authority, politicians, bankers and other substantial groups that were trying to do the people's will. Mob rule!! When you have politics controlled by intimidation, fear, threat and other tactics that reminds one of another period in the South, you and your government will end up in a totally different place than where the founders - the framers of the constitution – intended!!! They knew all too well and specifically warned us about this in those early writings. The constitution was framed with all intent to avoid just such a situation. They lived through enough of that before they left England and wanted NO MORE of it!!

ADDENDUM BASED ON RECENT EVENTS TILL 6/15/10

Now to the Tea Baggers. They have been led to believe it was done to them by the people who are stuck with the horrendous task of trying to fix the total damage done to them by the ReCorpiCons. They're willfully doing real damage to themselves by following these false prophets to their ultimate demise! They are following these RICH, SINFUL Judas Goats right off to their own slaughter! NOTE!

Oh, the things, the terrible things that have happened since this book was first published!! Just one of these horrendous disasters should clearly point to the awfully destructive agenda of the ReCorpiCons, but we have many, many to pick from to use as prime examples of this far too well progressed progression to total Fascism in America. To name a few, 29 killed in a mining accident, 15 killed in a refinery explosion and this stupid, stupid, easily prevented horrendous act in the Gulf of Mexico. Regulations as in other civilized countries could have and likely would have prevented these total calamities!!

One cannot but feel that SECRET MEETINGS, AGENDAS AND AGREEMENTS HAVE LED DIRECTLY TO THESE NEEDLESS LOSSES OF LIVES AND LIVELIHOODS FOR MILLIONS OF AMERICANS IN THE GULF REGION. Ironically, the loss of incomes is only the tip of the iceberg here. This is a total loss for many generations of 1/3 of America's seafood supply. It is a total loss of these beautiful coast lines and property values. It has or will totally destroy an entire important ecosystem for perhaps a century or more. It will negatively affect, for at least as long as 911, all of our lives and incomes and enjoyment or dining pleasures. It is a total, unmitigated, <u>preventable disaster</u> of a 911 101 magnitude <u>and should not be viewed in any way as the fault of the present administration</u> that has, by hapless timing, been tasked to try to mitigate or remediate the <u>disaster that was clearly caused by and for ReCorpiCon greed</u>. DO NOT LOSE THE POINT OF THIS FOCUS!! Katrina was, by contrast, an act of GOD – <u>not an act of a Corporation</u>! (Why is GOD blamed for all these naturally occurring bad things or disasters?) <u>WE'LL ALL BE DAMNED!</u>

Despite the cloud of HUBRIS here, <u>has no one else seen the total irony and hypocrisy</u>? When this and other "God" made disasters have occurred recently in the Gulf states why is it the ("States Rights" Federal Government Hating, reduce taxes, we're for Less Federal Government, the Big Government is wasteful and not good at doing anything, and who needs the big bad government?) spewing ReCorpiCon governors who are the <u>first to cry out when a Hurricane, Tornado, or ReCorpiCon caused disaster occurs to their state</u>, "<u>Where is the big bad government now that I need them</u>"? <u>Why aren't they here? Why aren't they doing more for us</u>? Why are they taking so long to get down here and bail us out? Why are they so seemingly non responsive? You have got to help us we are so desperate. All they can do is blame the big bad government – the very same government they want to reduce in size and effectiveness, by reducing taxes and cutting services. <u>YES, IT'S THE VERY SAME GOVERNMENT!!</u>

<u>THAT IS CLEARLY AN OXYMORON AND *EVERY* PUN IS DEFINITELY INTENDED HERE!!</u> THERE IS A REAL (I MEAN REAL) LESSON TO THIS. <u>The IRONIC TWIST. THESE SAME GOVERNORS ARE ALSO SUPPORTERS OF THE ReCorpiCons</u>

102 causing the disaster that has and will ruin their states both now and in the future. Oh yes, I recently heard from a Southern Senator that suddenly the military is one of the most efficient and well run organizations and should be brought to bear on this disaster. Is this not the same military that is part of this very same big bad horribly inefficient, inept government we've been told to hate? HEY GUYS, YOU JUST CANNOT HAVE IT BOTH WAYS!! IF YOU CUT THE TAXES THAT SUPPLY THE GOVERNMENT AND YOU ALLOW A WORLD WIDE MELT DOWN OF THE BANKS SO EVERYONE INCLUDING THE GOVERNMENT IS TAPPED TO THE BONE YOU CANNOT SUDDENLY EXPECT THEM TO BAIL YOU OUT WHEN IT HAPPENS TO BE YOUR TIME TO BE IN A DISASTER! START BLAMING THE RIGHT PEOPLE AND THE RIGHT SOURCES OF THESE DISASTERS. SAY WHAT YOU SAY TO THE POOR, "HEY, BUCK IT UP, AFTERALL, YOU ARE NOT ALONE, MILLIONS OF OTHER PEOPLE ARE SUFFERING RIGHT ALONG WITH YOU"! OH YEH, AND THAT SURE FIXES IT ALL!

HAD THEY REQUIRED THEIR ReCorpiCon friends and Corps put a sizable reserve into a fund to mitigate disasters like this and required them to install the safest possible processes to mitigate and protect against the "absolutely CERTAIN TO HAPPEN SOMETIME" disasters like this, the damaging results could have been kept to a minimum or totally non existent!! Oh, AGAIN, WE'LL ALL BE DAMNED!!!

WHEN IS AMERICA GOING TO WAKE UP AND SMELL THE OIL AND THE COAL DUST? WHERE ARE THE TEA BAGGERS NOW? THEY SEEM TO HAVE SLIPPED INTO THE OIL SLICK AND DROWNED. WHERE IS THAT "DRILL BABY DRILL" NOW? NOT SO POPULAR, IS IT? WAIT A MONTH OR TWO WHEN THE GULF BECOMES THE TOTAL DISASTER THAT IS NOW JUST

PREDICTED–IN THE MIDDLE OF THE TOURIST & FISHING SEASON!! THE TEA BAGGERS WILL BE LOOKING FOR AN OIL SLICK TO SLIDE UNDER AND DIE AS A MEANS TO AVOID SOMETHING FAR WORSE TO THEIR LIFE AND LIMBS.

YOU PEOPLE HAVE TO "PAY ATTENTION" TO YOUR OWN SITUATIONS AND USE YOUR OWN INTELLECTS TO SORT OUT THE PROPAGANDA THAT YOU HAVE BEEN FED FOR SO LONG and FIGURE OUT WHO has been FEEDING IT TO YOU AND WHY!!!! REMEMBER THE WALL ST. TYPES WHO RUINED YOUR SALARIES, HOUSES, SAVINGS, RETIREMENTS, JOBS, FUTURES AND THEN HAD THE BALLS TO HAVE YOU BAIL THEM OUT FROM YOUR NOW DEFUNCT POCKETS? AFTER YOU SPENT YOUR GRAND CHILDREN'S DIMES TO BAIL THEM OUT THEY HAD THE GOLD BALLS TO DEMAND THEIR HUGE SALARIES AND BONUSES TO REWARD RIPPING YOU OFF!!!

YOU SHOULD BE SO OUTRAGED THAT YOU WOULD BE PICKETING THEIR HOUSES EVERYDAY FROM NOW TILL FOREVER. I'M FRANKLY SURPRISED THAT SOMEONE HASN'T SCOUPED UP BARRELS OF THE OIL SLICK AND DUMPED IT ON TONY'S HOUSE. KEEP IN MIND, I DO NOT ADVOCATE THIS NOR DO I SUGGEST IT IN ANY WAY SHAPE OR FORM, BUT WHAT A POETIC, MENTAL IMAGE THAT PROVIDES AN EPIPHANY TO THE TONY'S OF THIS WORLD, THAT THEIR ACTIONS HAVE REAL AND VERY SERIOUS CONSEQUENCES FOR THEM AS WELL. BY THIS FICTIONAL FORM, THEY MAY BEGIN TO "GET IT" - THE TRUE CONSEQUENCES OF THEIR APPARENTLY RECKLESS, SEEEMINGLY IMMUNE, ACTIONS. "I NEED TO GET MY LIFE BACK" ISN'T THAT JUST PRECIOUS!!!!

What comes to mind is a MASH episode where Hawkeye shows a pilot - whose job it was to fly a plane and drop bombs on innocent people and then go back to base and a nice dinner with his wife and family – <u>some of the people he maimed or killed</u>. Till then the only thing he thought of was a nice flight and back to comfort. "A nice clean war" as the pilot put it. Somewhat like the Bankers and the oil company execs.! I'm also recalled to the way it was in the early days of industrialization where dangerous processes were involved and the owners took it very seriously. I recall seeing one of the DuPont estates built right over the gun powder works on the Brandywine River. He built his house right over the powder works so that he became part and parcel to any bad event that may occur at the gun powder plant and shared the risk of his employees. <u>That made it imperative for him to devise and install every safety process to prevent any such accident from happening.</u> <u>Guess what, it worked</u>!!!

Do you know the most remarkable thing is that the <u>ReCorpiCons after all this</u> and all that has happened <u>still claim that there is no need to regulate the Financial or the Energy industries</u>! Let them go Laissez Faire and just do their thing or what ever they feel like and hang the consequences <u>because they're too big and too powerful to be effected by it in any way shape or form</u>. THAT ATTITUDE MUST BE STOPPED AND STOPPED RIGHT NOW!!

<u>TEA BAGGERS</u>, THIS IS YOUR <u>ONLY CHANCE</u> TO <u>GET YOUR LIFE BACK</u> AND MAKE IT RIGHT FOR YOUR FUTURES AND THE FUTURES OF YOUR CHILDREN AND GRAND CHILDREN. STOP THE <u>PEOPLE WHO REALLY DID ALL THIS TO YOU</u>, INCLUDING THE HUGE DEBT (FROM A HUGE SURPLUS UNDER THE DEMOCRATS 10 YEARS AGO) <u>AND VOTE THE ReCorpiCons out</u>!!!! By the way, ReCorpiCons can be

Democrats as we all know of some in Arkansas and other states. <u>They clearly NEED TO GO AND NOW!!!!!</u>

Well, even though the title of this book is <u>DAMNED</u>, it could be "You'll be Damned" or "Y'all be Damned", or "Damn Lies". Regardless of what it is, the bottom line is <u>if you</u> - I mean everyone who can vote - <u>vote for the ReCorpiCons – and they are all easily recognized</u> – your <u>lives will be pure hell from then on</u>, because no matter what their names are, or what they say they believe <u>or claim that they will do for you</u>, THEY ARE NOT YOUR FRIENDS, NOR WILL THEY DO ANYTHING FOR YOU!! BUT THEY WILL SURE DO A HELL OF A LOT TOO YOU!! I MEAN THEY WILL DO REAL <u>DAMAGE TO YOUR LIFE</u>, YOUR EARNINGS, YOUR SAVINGS, YOUR WAY OF LIFE, YOUR HOUSE, YOUR RETIREMENTS, YOUR MEANS TO JUST LIVE OR GET BY!! <u>KISS EVERYTHING YOU LOVE AND TRUST GOODBY AS IT WILL GO OUT THE WINDOW.</u> <u>DO NOT BE FOOLED</u> BY THEIR SMILES, THEIR GLAD HANDS, <u>THEIR SMOOTH TALK</u>, <u>THEIR PROMISES</u> OF BEING A MAVERICK OR A CHANGE ARTIST <u>OR FOR YOUR COMMON GOOD. THEY JUST DON'T HAVE IT IN THEIR SOULS AND THAT ISN'T THEIR AGENDA!!!!!</u>

THE REALITY IS: THE <u>8 YEAR BLACK HOLE</u> IS THE <u>PREDICTOR OF THEIR INTENT</u> AND THE TOTAL DAMAGE THAT WAS DONE TO YOU AND YOUR LIVES AND INCOMES <u>IS A SIGN THAT THEY INTEND TO DO MORE OF IT</u>. <u>I GUARANTEE IT</u>. IT WILL BE <u>AT LEAST 10 TIMES WORSE</u> THAN <u>THOSE 8 YEARS</u> AS THEY'LL BE TOTALLY <u>EMBOLDENED</u> BY REGAINING POWER AFTER BEING SOUNDLY DEFEATED IN 2008. <u>GUARANTEED!!!!</u>

DO NOT LET THEM DO IT OR <u>Y'ALL BE DAMNED</u> AND <u>SUFFER THE MOST SEVERE CONSEQUENCES!!!!</u>

106   Let us now talk of JUSTICE and RULE OF LAW!! Do you think that JUSTICE IS EQUAL OR ADMINISTERED FAIRLY WITHOUT REGARD TO CLASS, OR LEVEL OF INCOME OR POSITION IN POLITICS OR A VERY LARGE CORPORATION? Boy, if you do, you have definitely come <u>under the spell of the most insidious ReCorpiCon propaganda machine since the early Forties in Europe</u>. If you do, you deserve every level of <u>HELL ON EARTH they INTEND FOR YOU</u> and BE ASSURED they'll meat out to you when they grab back power that <u>they ERRONEOUSLY FEEL that they DESERVE!!!</u>

If you ran a small company that inadvertently had an accident that killed even one person – let alone 11, do you think that you would be able to just walk away from that without any harassment, arrest or legal issues?

If you had not paid back taxes and owed even a SMALL fraction of say $100,000 in back taxes, do you think that you would be allowed to just come back later when caught and pay it whenever you could? <u>Y'll be damned!</u>

If you committed even a small crime – not even a crime against the government, constitution or the PEOPLE OF THESE UNITED STATES, do you think that just going public and saying, "Oh, I'm sorry, I guess I made a mistake" is going to get you off? <u>Not a bloody chance</u>!! NOT EVEN!!!

If you, by your reckless actions, caused a lot of other people in your neighborhood to lose their savings, their houses, their jobs or their retirements, that you would not only be able to just walk away, but in addition be amply rewarded for your recklessness and destruction of others

If you make a really inane statement in public that causes great harm or consternation so you go public and then apologize for having made an inadvertent misstatement even though you had fully intended and planned to say it, that everyone should just let you off the hook because you apologized? Y'ALL BE DAMNED!!

If you had an affair with someone that you were keeping very quiet and suddenly you are caught, so you go public and say, Oh, I'm sorry, I really hadn't intended to do that and I'll never do that again, that you should then be totally dismissed for your actions? Y'ALL BE DAMNED!!

Think about these recent and prominent examples and think how those who actually were involved in these things were let off easily or totally. Then think how it (JUSTICE) would have been for you and you get a total feel about HOW DIFFERENT IT IS FOR THOSE ReCorpiCons in Congress and in Corporations versus you and me! We get no breaks, we get no deference, we get no lea way and we get no leverage. THIS IS JUST ANOTHER CLEAR EXAMPLE OF HOW THE ReCorpiCons have taken over the government and made the rules to clearly benefit them at your expense. Taxes are just another example of this clear difference in treatment by the government. IF YOU DON'T GET THIS, THEN I FEEL VERY, VERY SORRY FOR YOU!!

THERE IS NO LEA WAY LEFT IN THIS EQUATION. THERE IS NO "PERHAPS, IF WE GOOF UP AND VOTE THE WRONG BUNCH INTO POWER", IT WILL ONLY BE FOR AWHILE, AND WE WILL GET IT RIGHT THE NEXT TIME!!! NO, NO. THIS IS IT!! THIS IS THE ONLY TIME LEFT AND IF YOU LET IT HAPPEN, Y'ALL BE DAMNED!! Y'ALL BE DAMNED FOR THE REST OF YOUR LIVES!

Let's talk about ReCorpiCons, vs. Right wing conseratives. Even though they have co-opted together as a matter of expedience for political reasons, they are clearly not the same entities, nor do they have the same principles, goals or interests in common. In fact they have so few in common, it is hard to believe that they can even get along or can talk to each other. It must be like forcing water into a pressure vessel at tremendous pressures – a situation that is bound to explode VIOLENTLY! (Water is not very compressible) Clearly, the ReCorpiCon agenda does <u>DAMAGE</u> to the Right Wing Conservatives. In fact it will inflict the very same <u>HELL on them</u> that it clearly has in mind for everyone else who is not really a ReCorpiCon. It must be like a SECRET SOCIETY where OATHS are taken, secret hand shakes and other symbols of authority, honor, loyalty and power are observed and repeated. Keep in mind, that ReCorpiCons have little conscience and only concerns for money – <u>lots of money for them</u>. <u>This clearly and absolutely goes against the principles of Christ or of any other religion, organized or not, that believes in a higher being or force that has the HIGHER GOOD FOR ALL basically as it's founding premise!</u> <u>Y'ALL BE DAMNED</u> IF YOU LET THEM WIN AND TAKE IT ALL AWAY FROM YOU - YOUR FREEDOMS, YOUR RIGHT TO BELIEVE AS YOU WISH AND TO CHOOSE YOUR OWN PATHS IN LIFE.

IT WOULD BE NICE TO SAY, OK, <u>IF YOU WANT TO BE DAMNED</u>, IT IS YOUR RIGHT TO DO THAT AND SUFFER FROM IT BECAUSE YOU WERE NOT ALERT ENOUGH OR CARING ENOUGH TO PREVENT IT FROM HAPPENING. <u>NO, THAT'S NOT GOOD ENOUGH!</u> MANY, MANY OTHERS <u>WHO CARED ENOUGH TO ACT WISELY</u> WILL BE <u>DAMNED WITH YOU!!!</u>

I SAID THAT ReCorpiCons are easily recognized. That is true, perhaps, for those who have been conditioned by years of ABUSE from ReCorpiCons and their agendas and thereby can recognize them immediately by their past ACTIONS and DEEDS and who they associate with most and who pays for their campaigns and how they vote, and not by what they say, what they claim, charming smile, their engaging life story, their popular images or their seemingly endless "just like you" folksy anecdotes.

10 CLEAR signs they are even REMOTELY ReCorpiCons. 1. They were the president or CEO of some large business, Corp. or bank, etc. 2. They had or have relatives that were in office who clearly stuck it to you and WE THE PEOPLE of US. A former shrub comes to mind. I knew from the first one that there was no way we wanted the 2nd one anywhere near that Office!! He wasn't elected either. 3. See who they gather around them as supporters or friends. 4. If they rally against unions in a state where they have no business they are the worst form of ReCorpiCon!! 5. If they call themselves progressives and "belong to the party" that tends to represent the PEOPLE, but BLOCK all legislation that would be for WE THE PEOPLE you instantly know they are ReCorpiCons. 6. Check who contributes most to their campaigns. 7. If they are normally part of the Hail, Hardy and Well Met crowd, they are absolutely ReCorpiCons. 8. If they can't put a sentence together that is more than 8 or 9 words – ie. a sound byte – they are definitely and absolutely ReCorpiCons. 9. If they are "Spokes Models" for a product called "running for office" they are clearly the worst possible Abhorrent ReCorpiCon as they are also just hollow shells spouting propaganda.

1 10 10.If they were an otherwise popular person like from the NBA, NFL, AFL, ACTORS, just a housewife or a hockey mom, they are very likely ReCorpiCons especially if they are also representatives of the Republican party. & White IF YOU FIND ANY OF THE CANDIDATES THAT COME ANY WHERE NEAR THESE ATTRIBUTES OR TRAITS, RUN THE OTHER WAY AS FAST AS YOU CAN. GENERAL RULE: IF THEY MADE OVER $100,000 A YEAR and/or PAY FOR A LARGE PART OF THEIR CAMPAIGN (Called buying the office) <u>YOU CAN REST ASSURED THEY DO NOT HAVE YOUR BEST INTERESTS IN MIND. EVEN A BAD DEMOCRAT IS FAR BETTER IN OFFICE THAN A REPUGNANT ReCorpiCon!!!!</u> Y'ALL BE DAMNED!!!

Well, there are probably at least 12 more, but I think that you now get it. However, if you fail to recognize them, and vote for them, <u>I'LL BE DAMNED, YOU WILL BE DAMNED WE'LL ALL BE DAMNED, Y'ALL BE DAMNED!!!!! FOREVER!!!!</u> AND IF IT HAPPENS TO YOU, DON'T COME CRYING BACK TO ME AS YOU <u>HAVE BEEN WARNED, YOU SHOULD HAVE PAID ATTENTION, TAKEN HEED and ACTED ACCORDINGLY!</u>

Once again, these unprecedented mine and oil events that have recently occurred <u>TELL THE WHOLE STORY NOW! Just like a car accident can ruin your life in an instant</u>, so can an earthquake, a hurricane, a tornado, an oil spill, Global Warming and there is nothing on earth that can fix it but <u>prevention or preparedness for the possibility</u>. It is called risk mitigation. <u>Prevention is REGULATIONS AND TRANSPARENCY – OVERSIGHT</u>. Preparedness is planning for contingencies and setting aside FUNDS and MEANS to deal with such tragedies if and when they occur at a moment's notice. <u>That is what a government is for</u>. Other wise, <u>I'LL BE DAMNED, WE' BE DAMNED, Y'ALL BE DAMNED!</u>